THE STORY
OF ENGLAND

THE STORY
OF ENGLAND

Christopher Hibbert

For John and Ursula, with love

PICTURE ACKNOWLEDGEMENTS

Royal Collection, St. James's Palace © Her Majesty The Queen. Windsor
Castle, Royal Archives © 1992 Her Majesty The Queen. Ashmolean Museum,
Oxford. John Bethell. Bibliothèque Nationale, Paris. Bodleian Library,
Oxford. Bridgeman Art Library. City of Bristol Museum and Art Gallery.
Britain on View (BTA/ETB). British Library, London. British Museum,
London. Burghley House, Lincolnshire. Cambridge University Library.
J. Allan Cash. Christ Church, Oxford. Mary Evans Picture Library.
Giraudon, Paris. Glasgow University Library. Guildhall Library, London.
Susan Griggs Agency. Sonia Halliday and Laura Lushington. Michael Holford.
Imperial War Museum, London. A.F. Kersting. Lanark Conservation Trust.
David Lyons, Event Horizons. Mansell Collection. Magdalene College,
Cambridge. Museum of London. National Army Museum, London. National
Maritime Museum, London. National Portrait Gallery, London. National
Postal Museum. Phaidon Archives. Popperfoto. Prado Museum, Madrid.
Public Record Office, Crown Copyright. Frank Spooner Pictures. Society of
Antiquaries. Homer Sykes/Network Photographers. Trinity College Library,
Cambridge. Victoria and Albert Museum, London. Dean and Chapter of
Westminster Abbey. Woodmansterne. Adam Woolfitt.

Phaidon Press Limited,
Regent's Wharf, All Saints Street, London N1 9PA

Phaidon Press Inc.
180 Varick Street, New York, NY 10014

www.phaidon.com

First published 1992
Reprinted 1992, 1993, 1994, 1995, 1997, 1998, 1999, 2000, 2002

© 1992 Phaidon Press Limited
Text © 1992 Christopher Hibbert

ISBN 0 7148 2652 9

A CIP catalogue record of this book is available from the British Library

Set in Linotype Sabon
Printed in Hong Kong

Contents

AUTHOR'S NOTE

In the introduction to his short history of England published in 1947, Professor E. L. Woodward remarked that an
attempt to cover so much ground in so limited a space was
like trying to pack the crown jewels into a hat-box: 'you can
do it only by leaving out the settings.' In this even shorter
account of the most influential people who have lived in
England during the many centuries outlined in its pages,
and of the most important events which have happened
during them, I have endeavoured to include as many of the
settings as I could so that the book might be lively as well as
informative, even at the cost of omitting certain themes for
which room might otherwise have been found.

It is intended as a generously illustrated introduction to
the history of England for all those readers who have largely
forgotten what they were taught at school, or whose history
lessons touched upon only parts of the long periods covered
here, as well as those looking for a readable book which will
help to put the places they visit in their travels about the
country into their historical context.

For readers in need of quick reference to facts, names and
places, the index has been made as detailed as possible and
includes the dates of birth and death of all the principal
people mentioned in the text. For further reference the
chronological charts folded in at the back of the book show
what was happening in the world at large as the history of
England unfolded. Specially drawn maps, showing all the
places mentioned in the text, castles, cathedrals, country
houses and battle sites, will also be found at the back of the
book together with the genealogies of English monarchs
and a list of Prime Ministers. Readers whose interest in
England's history is stirred by this brief narrative are referred to the bibliographical note on page 218.

Christopher Hibbert

THE BRITISH MELTING POT

From Neolithic times (5000-2500 BC)
to the defeat of the Anglo-Saxons (1066)

I

NATIVES AND IMMIGRANTS

5000 BC to 55 BC

One day towards the middle of the seventeenth century John Aubrey, a young law student at the Middle Temple, set out to explore the countryside around his father's estate in Wiltshire. Near the village of Avebury he came upon an extraordinary circle of huge stones which seemed to him to comprise an ancient monument 'as much surpassing Stonehenge as a cathedral doth a parish church'. Remarkable as the monument was and long as it had stood there, however, Aubrey's was the first detailed account of it. Even so, it aroused little interest. Seventy years later, in his *Tour through the whole Island of Great Britain* of 1724-6, Daniel Defoe did not consider Avebury worthy of remark; and, later on in the eighteenth century, when a local farmer decided to clear the ground for ploughing, several of the larger stones were pushed over into a pit filled with burning straw and smashed into fragments with sledge hammers. Stonehenge was treated less cavalierly; but it was not until recent times that any serious attempt was made to uncover the secrets of its history. Instead, tales were told of esoteric ceremonies, of priestly incantations, of human sacrifices upon the so-called Slaughter Stone.

Since Aubrey's day, while scholars have stripped some of the more fanciful myths from these ancient stones, the

Stone circle at Avebury,
Wiltshire, erected
c. 1800 BC.

reasons why they were so arranged remain a mystery, though the alignment of the Central Stone at Stonehenge with the Heel Stone – over which the sun rises on midsummer mornings – suggests a sanctuary connected with a sun cult. At least the monuments can now be dated with some accuracy. The Avebury stones were erected between 2000 BC and 1600 BC; the Stonehenge monoliths in at least five stages covering a span of nine centuries from about 2200 to 1300 BC. But of the people who placed them here, little more is known than of their purposes in doing so.

Prehistoric flint hand axe, found in Suffolk.

In the distant past, before the first monoliths were dragged across the open chalk down of Stonehenge from the mountains of Wales, that is to say seven thousand years ago, at the beginning of what was to become known as the Neolithic age, these and other areas of what is now England were occupied by roving bands of hunters who lived on the wild animals they could trap and kill, the fish they could catch in the rivers, or the wild plants they could pick. They grew no crops and had no livestock. Then, about six thousand years ago, these Stone Age hunters were joined by other peoples, immigrants from the Continent, small men and women, rarely more than 5ft 6ins in height, who crossed the sea in little skin boats, dug-out canoes and wicker-woven coracles, bringing with them a different way of life. They made clearings in the forests for their animals, grew crops, fashioned themselves axes and other tools from flint, baked pottery, and established meeting places and tribal centres such as that at Windmill Hill near Avebury whose summit was crowned by three concentric lines of earthworks. Followed by other immigrants, they developed the custom of burying their dead in stone tombs like that at West Kennett in Wiltshire whose finds are in the museum at Devizes.

Prehistoric pottery vessel of c. 3000 BC.

Among the new immigrants were the Beaker Folk who took their name from their distinctive bell-shaped drinking vessels with which they were buried in crouching positions in individual graves. These people, originally perhaps from

13

Spain, came from the areas now known as Holland and the Rhineland, bringing with them a knowledge of working in bronze. They arrived towards the end of the late Neolithic period and the beginning of the period known as the early Bronze Age in about 2000 BC, and seem to have settled down amicably with the earlier immigrants. It was they who were responsible for bringing the immense stones from Pembrokeshire in South Wales for the second stage of the building of Stonehenge, probably shipping them across the Bristol Channel and up the river Avon on rafts, then hauling them up to the site from the banks of the river at West Amesbury on tree trunks serving as rollers.

Other smaller waves of immigrants followed the Beaker Folk; but the population of the island remained small and its settlements widely scattered until, for reasons not yet understood, in about 1600 BC thousands more people appeared. More and more settlements were built on the hills over the downlands; agricultural land was laid out in immense field systems surrounded by groups of hut circles. The population, it has been estimated, rose to about one million by 1500 BC when, at the beginning of the late Bronze Age, yet other immigrants arrived, bringing with them skills and ornaments of a quality which had never been seen in the island before and which were to be collectively known as the Wessex Culture. These newcomers were traders as well as craftsmen, builders as well as, when necessary, warriors. As the Beaker Folk had done before them, they turned their attention towards Stonehenge; and, in the third stage of its building, dismantled the circle of stones erected by their predecessors, then dragged eighty immense blocks of sarsen stone from the Marlborough Downs to set them up, squared and dressed with their shaped lintels, in the circle and horseshoe of trilithons which still stand today.

Diverse as the people in the island already were, their stock was to become more varied still when in about 800 BC, at the beginning of the Iron Age, other settlers arrived

Defensive earthworks at
Hambledon Hill, Dorset.

from the Continent, at first in small groups then in larger bands. These were the Celts, a taller fairer race than the people who had come before, members of tribes which had long been settled in present-day France, Belgium and southern Germany and which were now moving west, retreating from more warlike tribes harassing them from the east. According to Gildas, the Celtic monk who was one of Britain's earliest historians, the Celts were 'completely ignorant of the practice of war'. In fact, their fighting men were armed with iron swords and daggers and their chieftains drove two-wheeled war chariots which were buried with them.

In the country they called Albion they built fortified hill forts with turf and stone ramparts, good examples of which can be seen at Maiden Castle in Dorset – which covers 115 acres and at one point has no fewer than eight lines of defence – and Cadbury Castle in Somerset, formerly a Neolithic settlement and occupied almost continuously for forty centuries. From such forts as these, and from other strongholds protected by water rather than ramparts – like

15

Glastonbury which stood on an island surrounded by swamps – Celtic tribesmen raided nearby settlements and carried off prisoners as slaves.

But the Celts were not essentially a bellicose people; even their chieftains seemed to have preferred hunting to war, while lesser men and women devoted their energies to husbandry. They were practised farmers, dividing the land into square fields separated by banks and working the earth with small ploughs drawn by oxen. They grew oats and rye, wheat and barley. Corn was ground in handmills for bread; and the alcoholic drink known as mead was made from water and fermented honey. They lived in round huts of wood and clay-covered wattle with thatched roofs. Both men and women wore brightly coloured clothes, red being a favourite colour, the material being dyed with a substance extracted from cockles. They had shoes and sandals of leather; and those who could afford them wore finely crafted ornaments and jewellery, brooches, bracelets, necklaces and rings, some of them made by their own people, others imported – together with glassware and wine – from foreign lands to which hides and slaves, cattle, dogs and minerals, tin from the mines of Cornwall, iron from Sussex, as well as gold and silver, were sent in return.

Celtic 'Battersea Shield' of beaten bronze, early 1st century AD.

Among the most industrious and virile of the Celtic tribes were the Belgae who had begun to immigrate to Britain from the valley of the Marne towards the beginning of the first century BC. They settled at first in the south-east, where they soon became the dominant people in the area; and, as their coinage testifies, they established centres at Colchester, St Albans and Silchester. One of the most powerful of their chieftains was Cassivellaunus, uncle to Cunobelinus, Shakespeare's Cymbeline, who ruled over a large area north of the Thames in what is now Hertfordshire, Buckinghamshire and Berkshire.

Kings like Cassivellaunus were far from being the barbarians of Roman propaganda. They were skilled administrators, patrons of artists whose beautiful curvilinear, abstract art decorated not only war shields and the hilts of swords but the backs of bronze looking-glasses and the lids of jewellery boxes. Certainly, when they made their appearance on the field of battle, they presented an awesome sight in their chariots surrounded by warriors wearing no armour, their hair long, their naked bodies dyed with woad. Yet for most of the time their people seem to have lived at peace with one another, marrying not only within their own tribes but with descendants of men and women who had come to Britain long before them. They learned about gods and the transmigration of souls from the wise men, astrologers and soothsayers known as Druids who worshipped and performed their rites in woods by the light of the moon beneath bunches of mistletoe clinging to the branches of oaks. According to Julius Caesar, the Druids offered up human sacrifices to their gods, sometimes single victims, at other times groups of men in immense wickerwork cages, criminals when these were available, slaves or poor men when they were not.

Fragment of Roman scale armour from Newcastle upon Tyne.

Previous page:
Mosaic pavement from the Roman villa at Fishbourne, Sussex.

Bronze head of Emperor Claudius, AD 41-54, found in Suffolk.

Julius Caesar, the great Roman general, invaded Britain for the first time in 55 BC, partly to gather information about the island of which so little was then known and partly to punish the Belgae who had helped their fellow tribesmen in their fight against the conquering Romans in Gaul, the land that is now France. He landed in Kent with several thousand men, although the soldiers in one of his legions had threatened to mutiny when told they were to invade the cold and misty northern island reputed to be full of savages wilder even than the Gauls. Strong tides prevented Caesar's cavalry from getting ashore; so, after some skirmishes in which the Romans took measure of the island which they were to call Britannia, he decided to withdraw. He returned the following year; and, although his sailors once again experienced difficulties with the treacherous waters of the Channel and several of his ships were badly damaged as they lay at anchor in a storm, he marched as far as Wheathampstead in Hertfordshire, Cassivellaunus's hill fort, which he captured after fierce fighting. He then withdrew with hostages and prisoners, having extracted an undertaking from Cassivellaunus and other British chieftains that they would pay an annual tribute to Rome.

Caesar returned to Rome with the knowledge that Britain was far from being the primitive island of brutal tribesmen which Romans had previously imagined it to be. It was not, however, until AD 43, after the death of the Belgic chieftain, Cunobelinus, that the Emperor Claudius decided to incorporate it into the Roman Empire. There was fierce resistance to the Roman legions which, having landed at Richborough in Kent, were brought to battle by Cunobelinus's son, Caractacus, by the banks of the Medway river. But, brave as they were, the Britons could not withstand the might of Rome. Defeated, Caractacus fled to Wales where, years later, he was captured and with his family taken in chains to Rome. After his defeat other British chieftains accepted the impossibility of successful resistance and submitted to the Emperor. Cogidubnus, chief

20

of the Regni, did so, for instance, and was duly rewarded, having Roman titles bestowed upon him by the Emperor and accumulating great wealth.

The Iceni of East Anglia also submitted at first; but when their chief, Prasutagus, died in about AD 60, bequeathing his property to the Roman Empire jointly with his two daughters, his wishes were disregarded by the Romans, who refused to accept Prasutagus's widow, the tall, red-haired, harsh-voiced Boudicca, as queen. When she insisted upon the recognition of her rights and those of her family, she was flogged and her daughters were raped. The enraged Iceni, assisted by the neighbouring tribe of Trinovantes, swarmed down towards the Roman town of Colchester, massacred its inhabitants, sacked the recently constructed temple and other buildings associated with the alien Roman rule, and routed the 9th Legion which had arrived from Lincoln too late for the town's defence. Then, led by Boudicca, the Britons turned south for the Thames and within a few days their rough and massive army was looking down upon the port of Londinium, then an unde-fended trading centre whose warehouses, shops and taverns, a few of ragstone and tile but most of wood and thatch, all lay open to attack. The destruction of the port was swift and complete. As at Colchester, its inhabitants were massacred and their buildings engulfed in flames. Boudicca's triumph, however, was short-lived. Faced by the power of a vengeful Emperor, there could be no final victory; and, rather than fall into the hands of her enemies, she took poison and joined the countless thousands of dead.

London was rebuilt, grew and prospered. By the middle of the third century, when it had become the administrative as well as the commercial capital of the Roman province of Britain, it contained perhaps as many as 30,000 people. Fifty years later there may have been almost twice that number, living in a semicircular area of 326 acres enclosed by three miles of strong stone walls, pierced by gates where the main roads entered the city and strengthened by bas-

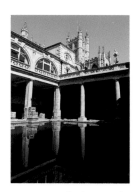

Roman baths at Bath, Avon, the spa of Aquae Sulis.

tions and towers. Elsewhere in Britain, as recalcitrant tribes were gradually conquered and pushed back towards the frontiers of Wales and Scotland, the Romans built other large towns, with temples and basilicas, barracks and public offices, amphitheatres, baths and workshops.

Most of these towns were arranged on the Romans' favourite grid-like plan which can still be recognized in the layout of the centres of Chichester (Noviomagus) and Gloucester (Glevum). In the north was York, then known as Eboracum, originally the headquarters of the 9th Legion. On the northern borders of the Welsh Marches was Chester (Deva), headquarters of the 20th Legion. Other cities were developed on the sites of old British settlements. Among these were Lincoln (Lindum), St Albans (Verulamium) and Silchester (Calleva), whose Roman walls still stand in places up to fourteen feet high. Other towns were developed as spas, most notably Bath (Aquae Sulis) whose baths and temple, now fully excavated, were revealed when the city was rebuilt during its eighteenth-century heyday. Yet others were constructed upon virgin sites, as, for instance, Exeter (Isca Dumnoniorum). Between these towns the Romans constructed a network of major and secondary roads, not always as straight as tradition would have them but of remarkable solidity as the surviving road across the moors at Blackstone Edge, Littleborough, still testifies. From London, roads radiated all over the country along routes which for much of their length are still in use as modern thoroughfares: to the north by way of Watling Street and Ermine Street; to the east by way of the Colchester road; to Chichester in the south by Stane Street; to the west by the road that passed through Silchester then on to Cirencester (Corinium) and Gloucester.

Just off this road, at Chedworth, Gloucestershire, are the well-preserved remains of a Roman villa, one of many which Romanized Britons occupied during the days of the Empire. Over six hundred of these Roman villas have now been unearthed, ranging from quite simple one-storey build-

Wall painting from a
Christian chapel in the
Roman villa at
Lullingstone, Kent.

ings to large houses of stone and slate, and splendid palatial
residences like the villa at Fishbourne which was probably
occupied by the Romanized Celtic King Cogidubnus. And,
from the objects dug up on their sites and in their surrounding farms, it has been possible to reconstruct the pleasant
life then enjoyed by the well-to-do under the protection of
Roman rule. Togas seem to have been worn in the Roman
fashion and shoes or sandals of leather. In cold weather
rooms, attractively furnished and handsomely decorated
with porphyry and marble, bronze ornaments and terra-
cotta figurines, were kept warm by heated flues beneath
mosaic-patterned floors. In those rooms where meals were
eaten there were blue and amber glass dishes and bowls,
silver plates, knives and spoons, oil lamps and candlesticks.
In bedrooms there were mirrors and boxwood combs on
dressing-tables, ointment jars and scent bottles, ear-picks,
skin-scrapers and manicure sets, pots of rouge, earrings and
bracelets. There were pens and ink-wells for writing letters,

Roman glass jug and
ribbed bowl of the
1st century AD,
found at Radnage,
Buckinghamshire.

23

Silver vessel, part of what is probably the oldest set of church plate from the Roman world.

dice and counters for playing games. Wine (better than the local fermentations) and olive oil were imported from the Continent, carpets from Egypt, silk, pepper and spices from the East. Latin was the official language; and most well-educated people spoke it as well as Celtic which remained the language of the poor, though many Latin words were incorporated into it.

For over three hundred years Britain remained a relatively untroubled outpost of the Roman world, the barbarians from beyond the frontiers of the Empire being kept at bay by forts and legions along coasts, at Branodunum (Brancaster) on the east coast, for example, and Anderida (Pevensey) in the south, and in the north by Hadrian's Wall, a great defensive barrier with a castle every mile, which was constructed on the orders of the Emperor Hadrian on a visit to Britain in about AD 121. Stretching seventy-three miles from shore to shore across bracken-covered moors from the Tyne to the Solway, it remains the most impressive surviv-

The 73-mile long Hadrian's Wall, built across the northern moors in c. AD 121.

ing Roman landmark in the country.

Overrun and partially demolished by tribesmen from the north in 368, the Wall was again attacked in 383 and the sentries in its turrets and the soldiers in its forts were slaughtered out of hand. By now the Empire itself was beginning to crumble into ruins; and in Britain one legion after another was recalled to fight Rome's wars on the Continent until by the middle of the fifth century Rome's protection was at an end. The islanders were left to fend for themselves.

Previous page:
The Bayeux Tapestry,
embroidered soon after the
Norman Conquest of
England in 1066.

The enemies of the Romanized Britons closed in upon them from every side. Fierce tattooed tribesmen rampaged down from Scotland; other marauders sailed across the turbulent Irish Sea in their light skin-and-wood boats called curraghs, massacring the farmers and fishermen along the western coasts; while, surging through the waters of the North Sea, came the shallow-draught ships of the Saxons, users of the *seax* or short-sword, and their northern neighbours, the Jutes, who fished and farmed in what is now southern Denmark, and the Germanic tribe, the Angles, who were to give their name to the English people.

Fair men with long hair and beards, clothed in thick, coarse shirts and trousers, in cloaks to which skins were sewn by their women to give them extra warmth when they were used as blankets at night, these raiders from across the North Sea carried iron-spiked spears, battle-axes and round wooden shields covered with hide as well as short-swords. Ruthless, violent men exulting in their animal energy, driving their victims before them like terrified sheep, as their war horns and savage shouts spread terror along the coasts, they pillaged and looted, raped and murdered, then sailed home again to their homes on the Continental mainland. But soon, tempted by the good farmlands of Britain, they began to settle in the island, establishing small communities of rough huts around the wooden halls of their thanes.

In 446 the Britons made a final, forlorn plea for help from Rome; then, since no help was forthcoming, they turned – or so it seems from the confused and incomplete records of these times – to a powerful chieftain, Vortigern, who proposed bringing over as mercenaries a strong Saxon war party. These men, led apparently by two Jutish chiefs named Hengist and Horsa, established themselves on the Isle of Thanet, an area of rich farmland off the Kentish coast. At first all went well; but then the settlers, calling over friends and reinforcements, demanded more and more land and more generous payments until at length the quarrels between them and the Britons flared into open war. The

Britons were defeated; the Saxons advanced; and, according to the Venerable Bede, the Northumbrian monk whose *History* is our chief source of knowledge for this period, the countryside and towns were alike devastated: 'None remained to bury those who had suffered a cruel death. A few wretched survivors captured in the hills were butchered wholesale, and others, desperate with hunger, came out and surrendered to the enemy for food, although they were doomed to lifelong slavery even if they escaped instant massacre. Some fled overseas in their misery; others, clinging to their homeland, eked out a wretched and fearful existence.'

The 8th-century Northumbrian historian, Bede, at work in his monastery.

This description is probably too highly coloured in its picture of woeful desolation; but certain it is that these were cruel times and that, rather than endure them, several families escaped across the Channel to the old Roman province of Armorica in the first of three stages of migration which eventually gave a Celtic language as well as the name of Brittany to this Atlantic peninsula of France. Other families apparently escaped to the west of Britain where a tribal leader named Ambrosius, evidently of Roman descent, offered shelter to the fugitives and to all those prepared to take up arms in defence of the old culture.

While the invaders continued to advance – one band of immigrants settling down in the kingdom of the South Saxons, which has given its name to the present-day county of Sussex, others establishing the kingdoms of the East Saxons (Essex) and of the West Saxons (Wessex) – further to the west along the borders of Wales and in Dumnonia, the peninsula occupied today by the counties of Devon and Cornwall, Roman Britain contrived to survive.

According to Gildas, a sixth-century chronicler who emigrated to Wales from Scotland where his father's estates were being constantly overrun by Pictish marauders, the Romanized Britons and British tribes threatened by the Saxon invaders flocked to Ambrosius's banner 'as eagerly as bees when a storm is brewing'. Presumably to protect themselves from the foreign marauders, and their cattle from raids by other British tribes, they built a series of earthworks, among them the Wansdyke, a massive ridge that stretches fifty miles from Inkpen in what is now Berkshire, across Savernake Forest and the Marlborough Downs to the Bristol Channel; and, behind this earthwork, they seem to have withstood attack and even to have won the occasional battle. It was at this time that there arose the legend of the mighty King Arthur, champion of the British, noble knight and courageous warrior, who, as Ambrosius's successor, stood firm against his people's enemies. He fought twelve great battles against the Saxons, so the Welsh monk Nennius recorded, and 'in all these battles stood out as victor'.

Whether or not King Arthur lived it is impossible now to say. But that there came to the fore at this time a British cavalry leader of extraordinary prowess there seems to be little doubt; and of the power and fascination of the Arthurian legend and of his Round Table of heroic warriors there can be no doubt at all. Places named after him can still be found the length and breadth of the country: no other name in Britain is encountered so often, except that of the Devil. And from time out of mind the site of Camelot, King Arthur's court, has been identified as that of a yellow sandstone hill, Cadbury Castle, which rises in the heart of the quiet gentle countryside of Somerset. Here in recent years have been discovered fragments of pottery similar to those unearthed at Tintagel in Cornwall – where King Arthur is supposed to have been born – and splinters of glass of a type imported from the Continent in the sixth century as well as the outlines of what seems to have been a large feasting hall of the same date.

The last of the twelve victories ascribed by Nennius to King Arthur, 'Commander in the Battles', was apparently fought between 490 and 520 at Mount Badon which is believed to have been somewhere in Dorset or Wiltshire. This great victory, in which 'nine hundred and sixty men fell in a single onslaught of Arthur's,' apparently brought peace for a time. But the encroachment of the Saxons across the island could not finally be resisted; and, before the end of the sixth century, Roman Britain was all but forgotten as Anglo-Saxon England began to take shape.

In the north the kingdom of Northumbria – one of the seven kingdoms, or Heptarchy established by the Angles and Saxons – extended its boundaries to the west; while, in the Midlands, the kingdom of Mercia assumed control over tracts of land so vast that by the end of the eighth century its ruler, King Offa – who built the great earthwork known as Offa's Dyke along his western borders to keep out the Welsh – controlled for a long time virtually all central, eastern and south-eastern England. In the south the kingdom of Wessex took control of Devon and Cornwall as well as the lands of the South and East Saxons; and, at the beginning of the ninth century, under their King, Egbert, the West Saxons defeated the Mercians and even laid claim to authority over the lands north of the Trent. When the Northumbrians submitted to him and took him for their master in 829, Egbert could reasonably consider himself overlord of all the English.

Offa, King of Mercia, from a painting in St. Albans Cathedral, whose Abbey he is said to have founded.

The confederation of the different kingdoms was a very loose one, though; and Egbert's dominion over it was far from secure. He had no central government and no means of raising an army well disciplined enough to defeat England's new enemies from overseas. These were the Northmen, Norwegian Vikings and Danes, tall fair warriors and pirates, as hungry for land as the ancestors of the English had been four centuries before. At first they came as raiders in their high-prowed ships, ravaging and looting along the coasts, sailing home to winter in their *fjords*. But then they came to settle, sailing up the Thames, wading ashore in East Anglia and on the coasts of Northumbria, pagan men as ready to beat in the skulls of defenceless monks as to cut down the English farmers who were assembled in their fighting forces known as *fyrds* to resist the

A page from the Gospels illuminated on the island of Lindisfarne in the early 8th century.

approaches of what the Anglo-Saxon chroniclers described as the 'great heathen host'.

Christianity had come to England long before. Towards the end of the sixth century, Ethelbert, King of Kent, had ridden from his capital to the coast to meet Augustine, the Prior of St Andrew's Monastery in Rome, who had been sent by the Pope to convert the heathen English to Christianity. Afraid of the stranger's magic, the King had received him in the open air but, soon persuaded by his sincerity, he had allowed him to preach to his people and within a few months Ethelbert had become a Christian himself. He provided Augustine with a house for his followers in Canterbury and in 597 allowed him to be consecrated Bishop of the English.

Seven years later another missionary from Rome, Mellitus, had been established as Bishop in London where King Ethelbert had built for him a church which was dedicated to St Paul. But Mellitus had found the staunchly pagan Londoners far more intractable than Augustine had found the people of Kent and, after the death of his royal patron, the men of London had driven their Bishop out of the city gates and had returned to their old religion and their former priests.

Christianity, however, was gaining a strong hold elsewhere in England where the gospel was spread not only by missionaries from the Continent and their followers but also by Celtic missionaries from Scotland and Ireland and from the holy island of Lindisfarne which St Aidan, a monk from Iona, had been given by Oswald, the Christian King of Northumbria. The missionaries who came from Rome held that the Pope's authority was supreme, the Celtic evangelists that Christian belief did not require a final earthly arbiter. There was little agreement between the two factions who differed even upon the calendar that settled the date for Easter; so in 664 a conference was held at Whitby in Yorkshire where a house for monks and nuns had been founded a few years before by St Hilda, great-niece of the

King of Northumbria. This Synod of Whitby decided in general favour of the Roman missionaries, foreshadowing closer ties with the Continent as well as the organization of the church into bishoprics, largely unchanged to this day, by such Christian leaders as the Greek, St Theodore, who was appointed Archbishop of Canterbury by the Pope in 668 and who called the first Council of a united English Church in 672 at Hertford, a demonstration of ecclesiastical unity that served as a model for a political unity not yet achieved.

As Christianity spread in England, churches were built all over the island. Most were constructed of split tree trunks which have long since disappeared but some were of stone, among them the original church of All Hallows by the Tower, the Northamptonshire churches of Brixworth and Earls Barton, and the little early eighth-century church of St Laurence, Bradford-on-Avon. Monasteries and abbeys were also being built, minsters, chapels and oratories; and

The Saxon church of St Laurence, Bradford-on-Avon, Wiltshire.

as the Church received bequests and grants of land so its riches and influence grew year by year.

It was this increasingly Christian England, slowly evolving into a unified state, which was threatened by the Vikings and the Danes who, well established in the north, were by the middle of the ninth century posing a threat to the Saxon kingdom of Wessex whose capital was at Winchester.

Here a remarkable young man had come to the throne in 871. This was Alfred, scholar, lawgiver, warrior and king, the first great statesman to emerge clearly from the mists of early English history. Of his physical appearance little can be said with confidence, but his biographer and friend, Asser, Bishop of Sherborne, painted a portrait of a man of exceptional gifts, devout and humane, devoted to the welfare of his people, as brave in battle as he was studious in scholarship, always careful to make the best use of his time so that he could continue with his studies and translations without neglecting the cares and duties of government, even inventing a water clock to help him in this endeavour.

In battle against the Danes at Ashdown in the Berkshire hills Alfred fought 'like a wild boar'. But, although his enemies were here defeated, the Danish incursions into England were soon resumed; and for a time Alfred, with a small company of faithful followers, was driven into hiding from the invaders on the Isle of Athelney in the Somerset marshes, moving 'under difficulties through woods and into inaccessible places' and giving rise to the famous legend that he sought shelter in a cottage where a woman scolded the unrecognized fugitive for allowing her cakes to burn by the fire.

Anglo-Saxon ring belonging to King Alfred's sister.

Gradually, however, the number of his supporters increased; and by 878 Alfred was able to bring the Danes to battle once more and to defeat them decisively. He obliged them to remain within an area bound by Watling Street known as the Danelaw, and persuaded their leader, Guthrum, and several of his leading warriors, to be bap-

Illustration from an 8th-century prayer book showing the biblical King David and his musicians.

tized as Christians. Taking advantage of the temporary peace, Alfred reorganized the *fyrd*, satisfying the complaints of men who had had to leave their farms for indeterminate periods to serve as soldiers; and he built up a strong navy to patrol the English Channel, forcing many would-be invaders to turn their attentions to northern France where their settlements became known as Normandy, the land of the men from the north.

Alfred, left for the moment in peace, turned his own attention to the restoration of English Christian culture, repairing pillaged churches, founding schools, setting scholars to work on the compilation of histories and the translation of texts, himself translating Bede's *History* – which celebrates the English people as a chosen race – grieving that men 'in search of learning and wisdom' had taken to going abroad 'when once they had come to England in search of such things', and looking forward to the day when 'all the youth now in England, born of free men, who have the means they can apply to it, should be devoted to learning'.

When Alfred died in 900 England was united as never before. By saving his own kingdom from the Scandinavian threat, he had given encouragement to others and had made

The 10th-century charter of Winchester Minster shows King Edgar offering the charter to Christ.

35

A helmet from the burial ship of an Anglo-Saxon king found at Sutton Hoo, Suffolk.

the West Saxon cause the cause of England. His successors did what they could to continue his work. His son, Edward the Elder, as skilled a soldier as his father though not so dedicated a scholar, and his formidable daughter, Ethelfleda, wife of Ethelred of Mercia, who ruled that kingdom after her husband's death as 'Lady of the Mercians', kept the Danes at bay and constructed a system of defences by building *burghs* or fortified settlements later to be known as boroughs, at strategic points, including Bakewell in Derbyshire, Tamworth and Stafford, Hertford and Warwick. Edward's son, Edmund, and his grandson, Edgar, gradually realized Alfred's dream of a unified England. The Danelaw was reconquered and in 973 Edgar was not only accepted as King of the English by Saxons and Danes alike, but also acknowledged as their overlord by kings in Scotland and Wales. During the reign of King Edgar, 'the Peaceable', between 959 and 975 there was a late flowering of Anglo-Saxon art and culture as well as an increase in the number of monastic houses for both men and women under the direction of St Dunstan, the scholar, musician and craftsman, maker of organs, bells and metal-work, who became Abbot of Glastonbury in 940 and Archbishop of Canterbury twenty years later.

King Edgar's descendants were, however, ill-suited to the task of defending England from renewed Viking invasions.

The Danish King Cnut takes over the throne of England by force in 1016.

His eldest son, Edward, was stabbed to death while he was still a boy; another son, Ethelred, who was crowned by St Dunstan when he was barely ten years old, was to be nick-named 'the Unready' or 'the Ill-advised'. His willingness to buy off the invaders with bribes known as Danegeld angered his own people – who were heavily taxed to meet the cost of the payments – while failing to placate the Danes whose King, Cnut, took over the throne in 1016, incorporating England into a Scandinavian empire which included Norway as well as Denmark.

England prospered under Cnut, a firm, just ruler who took pains to conciliate the English, marrying Ethelred's widow and becoming a Christian, much to the pleasure of the monks of Ely who 'sang merrily as the King rowed thereby'. In his time Danes and Englishmen learned to live more amicably together – though the riches and power of Danish earls were the cause of much jealousy – and there began to emerge the counties of England as we know them today, an England divided into shires with shire courts and shire reeves, or sheriffs, responsible for administering laws as comprehensive as any in the early medieval world.

Most people still lived in country villages. But perhaps as many as ten per cent were now town-dwellers; and several towns, notably Winchester, Norwich and York, were growing fast, as were ports like Southampton from which the English exported their textiles, metalwork and food-stuffs, as well as the slaves and the hunting dogs for which they had long been celebrated. London's population had risen to about fifteen thousand.

It was natural that such a country should continue to attract the eye of foreign adventurers, despite the strong fleet that Cnut maintained by renewing the annual tax of the Danegeld. And after the short reigns of his two sons and the accession to the throne of Ethelred the Unready's son, the white-skinned, white-haired Edward – known because of his piety as 'the Confessor' – greedy eyes were turned to the kingdom of this indolent man who seemed more con-

Portrait of Cnut, who incorporated England into a Scandinavian empire.

A coin depicting King Ethelred, known as 'The Unready'.

An 11th-century illustration showing Edward the Confessor at a banquet with his nobles.

cerned with the building of a great Abbey at Westminster than with affairs of state.

As soon as it was learned that Edward was dying no fewer than four men laid claim to the English throne, the King of Norway, the Duke of Normandy, and two brothers of Edward's Queen, Edith, one of whom, Tostig, the deposed Earl of Northumbria, was living in exile in Flanders. The other of these two brothers was Harold Godwinson, the hereditary ruler or Earl of Wessex, who immediately took advantage of his rivals' absence from the country to have himself crowned in the new Abbey of Westminster on the very day that its founder was buried there.

Shortly afterwards Tostig's men invaded Kent, then sailed up the east coast to pour ashore in Lincolnshire. Defeated by local levies, Tostig retreated north to await the arrival of the King of Norway whose Scandinavian warriors were soon sailing up the Humber towards York. Informed of this second invasion, King Harold, who was in the south preparing to resist the expected attack from Normandy, rushed north, won a brilliant victory at Stamford Bridge and, leaving both his brother, Tostig, and the King of Norway dead, brought his exhausted troops back to the Sussex Downs to face the army of the Duke of Normandy who had landed his knights at Pevensey. On 14 October 1066 the two armies clashed in a hard-fought battle north of Hastings at Battle. Towards the end of the day Harold was killed, shot through the eye by an arrow as tradition supposes, then hacked to death by Norman knights, one of whom cut off his leg, an unknightly deed for which Duke William dismissed him from his service. Anglo-Saxon England perished with Harold's death.

The death of King Harold at the hands of the Normans, at Hastings, 1066, from the Bayeux Tapestry.

THE SHAPING OF
THE NATION

From the Norman Conquest (1066)
to the Peasants' Revolt (1381)

4 $\quad$ **NORMAN RULE** $\quad$ 1066 – 1154

William I, the Conqueror, the first of the Norman kings, depicted in the Bayeux Tapestry.

Previous page: Elaborate carving on the south porch of the 12th-century church of Kilpeck, Hereford.

William, Duke of Normandy, the Conqueror, was then nearly forty years old; but it is difficult to say much more about him as a man with any certainty. He seems to have been about five feet ten inches in height, far taller than his minute wife, very strong and rather fat with reddish hair and a harsh, guttural voice. He was violent, domineering, calculating and avaricious, a man to fear. But he was abstemious, a pious Christian and, illegitimate himself, a faithful husband.

Vikings by origin and Vikings still by inclination – so holds one side in a continuing debate – he and his followers invaded England to deprive the island's people of their liberty, to kill their brave and noble King Harold, 'the hero and the martyr of our native freedom'. This was the testament according to Professor E. A. Freeman whose classic *History of the Norman Conquest* was published in five volumes in 1870-9. Another eminent Victorian, Thomas Carlyle, proposed a different interpretation: the Normans dragged us out of our primeval squalor. For what had the English been before they came? 'A gluttonous race of Jutes and Angles, capable of no great combinations, lumbering about in pot-bellied equanimity'.

Modern scholars rightly warn us to be on our guard against the misconceptions of this ancient and persistent polemical tradition, to recognize both the achievements of Anglo-Saxon culture and the benefits, as well as the ruthlessness, of Norman conquest.

Certainly William was not prepared to be merciful in his subjugation of his English enemies. His claim to the English throne, endorsed by the Pope, was genealogically stronger than the claims of his rivals; and he was determined to enforce it, to overwhelm all those who refused to recognize that his victory at Hastings had turned England into a Norman kingdom. For the moment this kingdom was far from secure: the Earls of Northumbria and Mercia both declined to submit, retiring to the north with the idea of proclaiming King Edward's young nephew, Edgar, as King

Harold's successor; both the Archbishop of Canterbury and the Archbishop of York supported the proclamation of Edgar as Harold's rightful heir; King Edward's widow remained in control of the old West Saxon capital of Winchester; and the gates of London, the key to England's dominance, were closed against the Norman invader.

Understanding the importance of London, and accepting the difficulties of attacking so large and well-defended a town with the few thousand knights and archers he could lead against it, William decided to surround it. After setting fire to the wooden buildings in the suburb of Southwark on the south bank, he marched west into Berkshire, then northeast to Berkhampstead, devastating the countryside on the way; and once London had been isolated, his enemies, as he had hoped they would, submitted one by one, followed by 'all the chief men of London, and they gave hostages to him, and he promised that he would be a gracious liege Lord', a ruler who would treat them justly if they gave him their service. He entered London shortly before Christmas; and on Christmas Day he was crowned King of England in Westminster Abbey where the shouts of acclaim were mistaken for calls for rebellion by the Norman soldiers on guard outside who began killing English spectators.

In places the fight against the Normans long continued; and William, who went back to Normandy three months after his coronation, had to return to England to put down revolts occasioned by the behaviour of the more rapacious of his barons, the powerful magnates, mostly brutal men who from such evidence as has come down to us appear to have been distinguished by moustaches of a monstrous size sprouting on either side of their iron nose guards. On his return to England, William showed scant mercy: great tracts of countryside were laid waste, and towns as far apart as Exeter and Durham were made to suffer his wrath. In the north hundreds of square miles were devastated and whole villages destroyed. In revenge the English 'here and there lay in wait in woods and secluded places secretly to slay [the

Sheep rearing and wool production became England's leading industries in the early Middle Ages.

hated Normans] as opportunity might offer'. And in retaliation the Normans introduced a Law of Englishry which decreed that a corpse was to be presumed to be that of a Norman unless it could be proved to be that of an Englishman and, on that presumption, a heavy fine was to be paid by the village nearest to the place where the body had been found. No fines were levied for dead Englishmen. It was not until the end of the twelfth century that it became difficult to tell the difference between the one race and the other. By then they had 'lived so long together and [had] intermarried and become so intermingled' that contemporaries could 'scarce distinguish [any more] betwixt Englishmen and Normans'.

By then also the system of land tenure known as feudalism, already developing in Anglo-Saxon times, had become an accepted way of life. In accordance with this system, William had given his followers – Bretons and Flemings as well as Normans – large estates in England, all of which he was deemed to own personally, scattering the estates far and wide over the country, so that those who held them could not easily combine to rebel against the King. The barons and earls thus rewarded with this land became tenants-in-chief of the King, to whom they were obliged to swear loyalty and for whom they were required, when necessary, to perform military service with an appropriate number of knights. They were also required, when summoned, to serve on the Grand Council – the successor of the Witan, the council of the Anglo-Saxon kings – from which Parliament was eventually to develop. The tenants-in-chief retained as much of the land granted them as they wished, distributing the rest to knights as sub-tenants who in turn allocated parts of them to the men who actually worked the fields, either as freeholders or as serfs. These workers at the bottom of the feudal scale paid for their respective shares by serving their master when called upon to do so and by working in his own fields for stipulated periods. The freehold tenants were allowed to leave the land if they wished and to settle elsewhere; but the far larger number of serfs or villeins were tied to the land of their lord and, in most cases, could gain their freedom only by paying for it or by running away to a town where, provided they had not been recaptured within four days, a court order would be required to bring them back into servitude.

The record of land known as Domesday Book, completed in 1086, standing on a replica of the casket in which it was originally kept.

In order to have a reliable record of all his lands, his tenants and their possessions and to discover how much they could be called upon to pay by way of taxes, William ordered the compilation of the inventory of his assets known as Domesday Book, now to be seen in the Public Record Office. From this it appeared that in 1086 about half the cultivated land in the country was in the hands of 170 tenants-in-chief, only two of whom were English barons; about a fifth was held personally by the King and most of the rest by bishops and abbots and other heads of religious houses who paid for it by their prayers or by paying scutage, a tax which lay landholders also came increasingly to pay in lieu of knightly service.

To the English serfs who lived within their shadows, the most obvious symbols of the power of their new landlords and masters were the castles that now appeared all over England, no fewer than five hundred of them within a generation of the Normans' coming. Others were to be built with every passing year; there were to be forty in Kent alone. The earliest of them were usually of wood and quite simple in design. Constructed on an earthen mound, surrounded by a ditch, they comprised a tall tower enclosed on all sides by a palisaded rampart. The ditch was usually filled with water, and a drawbridge led across it to the castle's single gate. The great castle at Windsor and the Tower of London were first built in this modest way. As time passed, however, castles were required to serve not only as a means of overawing a disaffected and unruly people, as garrisons, supply bases and fortified centres of administration, but also as noble dwellings built of stone or flint or rubble faced with stone. They still had to be formidable fortresses with immensely thick walls, high towers and moats, and sometimes, as at Kenilworth, with a staircase on an outside wall leading to a heavy, well-protected door on an upper floor. But there also had to be sleeping chambers on the upper storeys, dining halls, chapels and, in the larger castles, a series of rooms known collectively as the wardrobe in which clothes were kept and valuable household stores, including expensive spices, were deposited in locked chests with jewels and plate. Such castles, ruined, restored or rebuilt, can be seen in every county, along the coasts at Dover and Bamburgh, in the west country at Launceston and Berkeley, in Sussex at Lewes and Arundel, along the Welsh Marches at Ludlow and Chepstow, in Yorkshire at Richmond, in the Midlands at Rockingham and at Oakham where there is a fine example of a Norman castle's great hall built like a church with a nave and two side aisles, since masons had not yet mastered the craft of roofing a wide span.

St Mary the Virgin, Iffley, Oxfordshire, one of England's finest late Norman churches.

Churches appeared even more ubiquitously than castles, for the population was rising rapidly and being divided into parishes, neighbourhoods within the counties which have survived virtually unchanged into our own time. There were relatively few people in the north which had been devastated so remorselessly in the years immediately following the conquest: in Yorkshire there were perhaps no more than thirty thousand people, and in the whole of the north probably no more than four people to the square mile. But few counties in the south had fewer than fifty thousand each. There were about seventy thousand in Devon, ninety thousand in Lincolnshire, and in Norfolk – the most populous county of all – nearly a hundred thousand. By the time of Domesday Book the population of England seems to have been approaching two million. Most of these people still lived in villages, since all but the five largest towns had less than a thousand inhabitants, and places where large towns were later to be built, from Portsmouth to Newcastle, and Liverpool to King's Lynn, were not yet even villages. Some towns, like Newbury in Berkshire, were recent Norman foundations; but most were Saxon towns growing slowly. St Albans, so populous in Roman times, and having well over seventy thousand inhabitants today, had just forty-six burgesses in 1086.

Yet, even in the north, builders were busily at work,

Durham Cathedral looking from the south aisle into the nave which was finished in 1188.

Tympanum of the Prior's Doorway in Ely Cathedral, perhaps the finest Romanesque doorway in England.

erecting new churches, reconstructing Saxon ones, employing the style of architecture known as Romanesque with its rounded arches favoured by architects of the Roman Empire, square towers and plain vaulting. The west front of the parish church at Iffley outside Oxford is but one splendid example of Norman architecture at its most satisfying and robust, the nave of Durham Cathedral but one such nave in an early English cathedral, the interiors of St Bartholomew the Great, Smithfield and St John in the Tower but two places of worship in London where the atmosphere of the Norman Church is powerfully evoked. Work on Durham Cathedral began in 1093. By then no fewer than fourteen of England's greatest cathedrals were already under construction; all the rest with one exception were started early in the next century. The one exception was Salisbury Cathedral which was not begun until 1220; but two miles north of Salisbury, at Old Sarum, a cathedral had been in existence since 1092.

William took a deep interest in the development of the Church in England, encouraging the efforts of the Italian-born Lanfranc – whom he had summoned from Normandy to install as Archbishop of Canterbury – to bring a characteristic Norman efficiency into the administration of ecclesiastical affairs and to take the English Church closer to Rome. Yet the King, for all his professed regard for the Pope and the Roman Church, took care to maintain his own independence: no bishop might visit Rome or even write to the Pope without his permission; no excommunications might be imposed in his large realm without his express consent. Although William's determination to be supreme in Church as he was in State often brought Lanfranc into dispute with the Pope, the Archbishop remained as loyal as he was devoted to the King; and when news was brought to him of the death of the Conqueror after an injury received while riding on the Continent, he was so prostrated by grief that his monks thought that he too might die.

Lanfranc's distress was exacerbated by his concern that the son whom William had chosen to succeed him was wholly unfitted for kingship. This son, also William and known as Rufus because of his florid complexion, was a short, fat, bull-necked man with a bitingly sarcastic tongue and a savage, bullying temper. He mocked the piety of churchmen, insulted foreign envoys and flaunted his homosexual tastes. One day he asked Anselm, the leading theologian of his day – who had been appointed Lanfranc's successor as Archbishop of Canterbury after a long delay during which the King appropriated the archiepiscopal income – what sin he would be condemning in his next sermon. Anselm bravely replied, 'The sin of Sodom.' The King laughed in his face.

While accepting money from malefactors who could afford to pay bribes to evade justice, William inflicted punishments on those who had offended against him with even greater severity than his father had done, blinding and castrating one rebel noble, and flogging the noble's steward by the door of every church in Salisbury before having him hanged. But to no malefactors was he more severe than he

A 13th-century illustration showing the four Norman kings of England – clockwise from top left, William I, William II, Stephen, Henry I.

was to those who offended against the forest laws, the scope of which he much extended.

His father had earned widespread hatred for his strict imposition of these fierce laws and for extending the boundaries of the royal forests which included tens of thousands of acres of land, by no means all of it wooded, over which the King and his friends could hunt deer. To preserve this pleasure for himself William I had poachers blinded and mutilated, and even those who gathered sticks on royal land were savagely punished. Disregarding the objections and pleas of rich and poor alike, he 'recked not of the hatred of them all, for they needs must obey his will if they would have life, or lands or goods'. In creating the royal game preserve known as the New Forest in Hampshire, which still today encompasses over 90,000 acres, he demolished dwellings and entire villages. Nor was the New Forest the largest of the royal forests: the whole of Essex was subject to the forest laws; so were immense tracts in the Midlands, around Windsor in Berkshire and in Oxfordshire where the hunting park of the Anglo-Saxon kings at Woodstock remained in royal hands until the beginning of the eighteenth century when Queen Anne gave it to the first Duke of Marlborough for the building of Blenheim Palace.

A 12th-century psalter depicts haymakers scything.

By the time of William I's grandsons, the royal forests had become so extensive that they may have covered almost a third of the country. A sizeable proportion of the rest of the land in England was enclosed as game preserves by the King's tenants-in-chief. Some of these preserves are still in private hands like Knowsley Park, the property of the eighteenth Earl of Derby. In others herds of red and fallow deer still roam between the rocks and bracken in the shade of ancient oak trees as at Bradgate Park in Leicestershire where stags and does were once hunted by the medieval Earls of Winchester.

In August 1100 King William II was hunting in the New Forest when he was killed by an arrow, shot either accidentally or on purpose. His companions disappeared and his body, dripping blood, was taken by local serfs in a cart to Winchester where it was buried in the recently consecrated Cathedral whose tower soon afterwards collapsed, a disaster attributed to the unworthiness of the intolerable King for Christian burial.

'All things that are loathsome to God and to earnest men were customary in this land in his time,' wrote an English chronicler; 'and therefore he was loathsome to all his people, and abominable to God, as his end showed, forasmuch as he departed in the midst of his unrighteousness, without repentance and without expiation.'

His younger brother, Henry, who had also been hunting in the New Forest that day, immediately appropriated the royal treasure and insignia and had himself crowned in Westminster Abbey without delay. A severe man like his father, he was avaricious and crafty as well as cold-hearted; he had a passion for slaying deer and was said to have callously thrown a prisoner from a castle tower into the waters of a river far below. But he was anxious to persuade the English people that the lawless days of his brother's time were over. He imprisoned the detested Rannulf Flambard, the Bishop of Durham, William's deeply unpleasant chief adviser, in the Tower of London; he called Anselm back to Canterbury from France where he had been exiled by William; he issued a proclamation to the people promising to observe their rights; he put a stop to the depredations of the royal bodyguard who in his brother's day had become notorious for their robberies and rapes during the progresses of the royal household and its officials, the effective government of the country. He frequently went on progresses himself, visiting as many parts of his kingdom as he could and keeping a sharp eye upon the barons whose loyalty to the Crown was not to be taken for granted. 'Great awe there was of him,' recorded a chronicler, 'No man dared misdo another in his time.' Able to read and write – accomplishments then mastered by few, even of the highest rank – he acquired a reputation for

Contemporary illustration of the sinking of the *White Ship* in which King Henry I's heir was drowned in 1120.

scholarship as well as for firmness of hand: men called him Henry Beauclerk.

He won much goodwill by setting an example, soon to be followed by other Normans of high rank, by taking an English wife, Matilda, who was descended directly from Alfred the Great. Already the father of numerous children by a succession of mistresses, he had a son by Matilda, a boy of whom he held high hopes; and when this 'goodly heir' was drowned at sea with the entire crew and all but one of the passengers of the *White Ship*, the fastest vessel in his fleet, the King is said to have fallen unconscious to the ground at the woeful tidings and, as every English schoolboy used to know, he never smiled again.

The boy's mother had by then died herself. The King married again; but by his second wife, daughter of the Duke of Lower Lorraine, he had no children, and so he decided to make the drowned boy's sister, Matilda, his heir. This young woman was nineteen at the time of her brother's drowning. She had been married to the Holy Roman Emperor at the age of twelve and after his death had married Count Geoffrey of Anjou. Most of the barons did

The Banqueting Hall of Hedingham Castle, Essex, where Queen Matilda died in 1152.

not take kindly to the thought of Matilda as their Queen. She had lived so long abroad that she seemed to them a foreigner; moreover they considered her far too autocratic and masterful for a woman. Indeed, in the opinion of one observer, Annulf of Lisieux, she was a woman who, apart from her undoubted beauty, had 'nothing of the female in her'. Many barons preferred the claims of Matilda's cousin, Stephen, Count of Blois – whose mother was William the Conqueror's daughter – an affable, apparently easygoing and generous man who made many promises to his potential supporters, offering them splendid rewards when he became King.

Stephen rushed over to England upon King Henry's death and was welcomed into London where his brother, Henry of Blois, the most powerful of the English bishops, persuaded the Archbishop of Canterbury to crown him at Westminster shortly before Christmas 1135.

Outraged by her cousin's breach of faith, Matilda, who was still in Normandy, appealed unsuccessfully to the Pope; then, having done her best to make trouble for Stephen in England, she landed in Sussex, travelled to Bristol where the barons of the West Country rallied to her support, and entered London in triumph. By then the English people, commoners and barons alike, had grown to resent Stephen's weak and erratic rule, the violence of his Flemish mercenaries, the power exercised by his influential Flemish adviser, William of Ypres, his scattering of the treasure which Henry I had accumulated, and his failure to abide by an oath to disafforest various royal lands. But Matilda was no better liked than Stephen. More arrogant and haughty than ever now that she was in control of the capital, she took the title of Queen without being crowned, appropriated lands to which she had no right, and when a deputation of the citizens of London petitioned for the observance of ancient laws she swore at them and drove them from the room. Soon afterwards she herself was driven out of London.

Silver penny piece, depicting King Stephen and his wife Matilda, issued in 1141.

The years of quarrelling and fighting during which Stephen and Matilda and their baronial allies struggled against each other for the throne were so horrifyingly described by a monk of Peterborough – who lived in the midst of an area of peculiar turbulence – that they have been taken as characterizing the whole of the 'nineteen long winters' when 'God and his angels slept.' The barons 'greatly oppressed the wretched people by making them work at their castles,' the monk of Peterborough recorded, 'and when the castles were finished they filled them with devils and evil men. Then they took those whom they thought to have any goods, both men and women, and put them in prison for their gold and silver, and tortured them with pains unspeakable.'

Certainly there did occur such horrors. Geoffrey de Mandeville, grandson of one of William the Conqueror's knights, who changed sides as often as he conceived it in his interests to do so and wrung all manner of rights and privileges, including the earldom of Essex, from the opposing sides, rampaged about the country on indiscriminate raids, pillaging and burning, taking hostages and exacting blackmail. But Geoffrey de Mandeville was mortally wounded by an arrow at Burwell in the summer of 1144; in 1147 recruitment for the Second Crusade drew many other adventurers out of the country; and at the beginning of the next year Matilda returned to Normandy, her cause lost. The worst troubles were then over. Stephen ruled for a further seven years until his death at Dover. Buried at the Cluniac Faversham Abbey, which he had founded, he was succeeded by the son of his rival Matilda and her second husband, who came to the throne as Henry II in 1154.

Royal seal showing King Henry II riding into battle.

Previous page:
The 13th-century stained glass window of the Magi in Canterbury Cathedral.

It was claimed by one of the men about his constantly peripatetic court that the hands of Henry II, the first of the kings of the House of Plantagenet, were never empty: they always held either a bow or a book. He was certainly addicted to hunting, which he pursued with a ferocious energy. At the same time he had more learning than any European monarch of his time. From his earliest youth he had been 'imbued with letters and instructed in good manners beseeming a youth of his rank'; and, by the time he came to the throne at the age of twenty-one, his Latin was as fluent as his French. He was said, indeed, to have a good knowledge of all the tongues spoken between the Bay of Biscay and the Jordan, though evidently not of English. He never lost his love of literature nor his taste for intellectual discussion which he would carry on far into the night after a long day spent chasing deer. He never seemed tired, nor ever satisfied.

He transacted all his business standing up, pacing backwards and forwards on bowed legs covered with sores from the saddle, fiddling with his hunting gear, 'beguiling with scribbling or with whispered talk the enforced tranquillity even of the hour of Mass'. He was short and thickset with reddish hair cropped very short and a coarse complexion blotched with freckles. His eyes were prominent and often bloodshot and appeared to change colour when he flew into one of his alarming rages which were so uncontrollable that he would throw himself to the floor and grind the rushes that covered it between his teeth.

Yet 'all folk loved him', according to an English chronicler, 'for he did good justice and made peace.' Certainly, much could be forgiven a man who showed himself so determined to bring the disorders of King Stephen's reign to an end. Nineteenth-century historians were in the habit of giving Henry II more credit for his reforms than is his due; and it has since been emphasized how far the legal institutions of the country had already progressed before his coronation in 1154; yet his achievements were nevertheless

The ruins of Bolton Abbey, Yorkshire, founded in 1120 near Skipton, and moved here in the middle of the century.

remarkable, particularly so as England was but one part of his extensive dominions, which stretched from the Loire to the Pyrenees, and he had to spend much of his time on the Continent. In England he plunged into the tasks that faced him with almost demoniac energy, dismissing the Flemish mercenaries who had plagued his subjects for too long, demolishing scores of castles which had been built in Stephen's time, strengthening and widening the powers of his sheriffs – officials now trained in the law who were responsible for military as well as judicial affairs in their respective shires – recovering royal estates and aggrandizing royal influence at the expense of overweening barons from whom he demanded money rather than military service, preferring to rely for armed support upon a militia composed of English freemen. As for the law, he encouraged the process, which had begun in the time of Henry I, whereby the jurisdiction of the king's courts and of the king's judges encroached upon that of the old courts whose hearings had been held in the hall of the local lord. There were large profits by way of fines and fees to be derived from jurisdiction, and the King was determined to reap them for himself. So cases which would formerly have been heard in the court of a local baron were now increasingly heard before royal itinerant justices who travelled about the country under guard, applying the law impartially at assizes and gradually establishing a common law in place of the customs of the manor which had previously varied not only from shire to shire but even from one community to another. Moreover, the jury system – whose origins can be traced to primitive trials in which witnesses were called forward to swear to the innocence of the accused – was at last replacing old English ordeals by fire and water and old Norman trials by battle.

Within the memory of men living in Henry II's time both these methods of determining guilt or innocence were still commonly practised. Indeed, trial by ordeal was not formally abolished until 1219. It took place in church, or in pits dug outside it, where fires were lit and bowls of water and bandages prepared. The witnesses, all of whom 'must be fasting and have abstained from their wives during the night', were sprinkled with holy water and given 'Gospels and the Symbols of Christ's Cross' to kiss. When the water was boiling the accused's arm was bandaged and he was required to plunge it into the bowl to pick out a stone lying at the bottom. After three days the bandages were removed. Evidence of scalding was taken to be proof of guilt. As an alternative to the ordeal by water, the accused might be required to pick up a red-hot iron bar and hold it in his bare hand while he walked three paces. His hand was then sealed by the priest and if after three days a blister the size of a walnut had appeared he was declared guilty.

In trials by combat, which were still occasionally taking place in the fourteenth century, the contestants were attended by three priests who sang a Mass on the day of the trial and blessed the harness and weapons before the fight took place. Women and the old and infirm were excused from fighting personally and were allowed to appoint champions on their behalf. So were priests. Priests were also excused trial by ordeal and were required instead to eat a piece of bread and cheese before the altar. A prayer was made to God to send down the archangel Gabriel to stop the throat of the priest if he were guilty. If he managed to eat the food he was presumed innocent. The clergy had other privileges, too: when accused of a crime they could be punished only in ecclesiastical courts and if found guilty there, while they might be unfrocked, they were more likely to be sentenced merely to suffer penances. In time this Benefit of Clergy came to be accepted as a plea against capital punishment in any court and could be claimed not only by priests and monks but by anyone accused of crime who could produce evidence that he was an educated man. The ability to read a few lines of a prescribed text – which illiterate prisoners often learned by heart with the help of accommodating gaolers – was taken as being sufficient evidence of education.

It was these exceptional privileges enjoyed by the clergy which brought King Henry into collision with the Church. His efforts to encourage a common law and to extend the scope of royal jurisdiction had not aroused much opposition from the barons, most of whom were happy enough to see the power of the more unpleasant of their number reduced for the sake of good order in the realm. But his attempts to have clergy who had been found guilty in ecclesiastical courts brought before civil courts for sentence, and to put a stop to appeals being made directly to Rome, angered the Church and led to his fateful quarrel with the Archbishop of Canterbury.

This Archbishop was Thomas Becket, son of a Norman merchant who had settled in London. A young man of exceptional gifts and striking personality, he had been appointed Chancellor of England, the King's chief secretary, before he was forty, the first man born in England to have held so high an office since the Conquest; and he had become so intimate a friend of the King that they were said to be inseparable. A year after Becket became Archbishop, a canon of Bedford was acquitted on a murder charge in the Bishop of Lincoln's court. The King demanded that the man

Contemporary illustration of the murder of Thomas Becket in Canterbury Cathedral in 1170.

63

should come forward to answer the charge in a civil court. Becket refused to allow this, countering with the demand that the King should come to plead his case in the ecclesiastical court at Canterbury. The dispute became more and more bitter until Becket thought it as well to go abroad. He spent six years on the Continent living an ascetic life – in marked contrast to the life he had formerly led at court and as the King's companion in the chase – threatening to excommunicate Henry and carrying out the threat against others whom he deemed to be enemies of the Church. Henry, who hated his former friend all the more because he had once loved him, retaliated by exiling all Becket's near relations and seizing his properties; and in 1170 he offered him a final insult, ignoring all precedents and defying the Pope, by getting the Archbishop of York to crown his eldest son as his partner in kingship. Fearing that he might have gone too far and that this defiance of the Church might provoke the Pope to prohibit Englishmen from participating in the sacraments, Henry allowed an agreement to be patched up and Becket returned to Canterbury. But soon fresh quarrels broke out; and Henry, while on a visit to his Continental possessions, was heard to burst out, 'What a parcel of fools and dastards have I nourished in my house that none of them will avenge me of this one upstart priest!' Four knights, taking the King at his word, and no doubt hoping for reward, sailed to England to murder the Archbishop. They came upon him in his cathedral and cut him down with their swords, the last blow splitting their victim's tonsured skull and spilling his brains on the stone floor of the north transept.

The body was buried next day in the crypt and almost immediately the grave became a place of pilgrimage, as it still was in and beyond Chaucer's time when, 'from every shires ende of Engelond', pilgrims wended their way to Canterbury, 'the holy blisful martir for to seke'. In 1173 the martyr was canonized and the following year the King thought it advisable to don pilgrim's weeds at Canterbury and do public penance for Becket's death, allowing himself to be scourged by all seventy monks of the chapter.

The remaining fifteen years of Henry's life were not happy ones. Soon after his marriage to Eleanor of Aquitaine, he had fallen in love with Rosamond, the daughter of Walter de Clifford, owner of extensive estates along the Welsh Marches; and his attachment to this beautiful girl – that 'masterpiece of nature' whom her lover, so legend relates, sequestered from jealous eyes in a tower within a maze at Woodstock – was at least partly responsible for his unhappy relationship with his wife who, from her court at Poitiers, encouraged her sons in their opposition to him. For years Henry was intermittently at war with these sons and their ally, the King of France, until in 1189, having lost Le Mans and all the principal castles of Maine, he was forced to agree to a treaty with them and to pay an indemnity to the followers of the eldest surviving son, Richard. The sight of the name of Richard's younger brother, John, in lists of those who had fought against him, was more than the King could bear. Already dying, he turned his face to the wall and murmured, 'Enough! Now let things go as they may. I care no more for myself or for the world.'

He died on 6 July and two months later Richard was crowned at Westminster. Brave, dashing and impulsive, with a taste for poetry, he seemed more like a romantic cavalry leader than a king, and from the first was unwilling to devote his attention to the government of England where, in a reign that lasted almost ten years, he spent scarcely more than four months. He had been born at Oxford; but he spoke French and considered himself French, regarding England as a useful inheritance on which to raise money. At the time of his coronation he had already undertaken to take part in the Third Crusade, and he now instructed his agents to scour the country for funds to equip himself and his knights and fleet with appropriate power and splendour, 'offering for sale all he had,' so it was recorded, disposing of royal property left and right, selling his half-brother the

Manuscript illustration of the enthronement of Richard I in 1189.

Illustration from the Luttrell Psalter of c. 1340 showing Richard I and the ferocious Saladin in combat in the Holy Land.

archbishopric of York and releasing the King of Scotland from his allegiance for ten thousand marks. 'I would,' he is alleged to have declared, 'sell London itself if I could find a purchaser rich enough to buy it.' He died as no doubt he would have wished in battle, killed by an arrow while besieging the castle of Chalus. In what was considered to be a characteristic gesture, he gave orders that the archer who had shot him should be spared; but, no less characteristically, the captain of his guard had the man flayed alive, and all his companions hanged, when the castle was captured.

John, who now succeeded to the English throne, bore no resemblance to his brother, either in character or in appearance, although he was attractive when he chose to be, particularly to women for whom he had an appetite as keen as his father's. Scarcely more than five feet tall, he was good looking with widely-set eyes, long curly hair and a neatly trimmed beard. But of his character little that was favourable was ever said. One Victorian historian described him as 'a monster of iniquity', another as 'mean, false, vindictive, abominably cruel ... frivolous and slothful ... self-indulgent and scandalously immoral ... At once greedy and extravagant, he extorted money from his subjects and spent it in an ignoble manner. He had a violent temper and a stubborn disposition, but he lacked real firmness of mind, and was at heart a coward ... While he was abjectly superstitious, he was habitually profane and irreligious.' It had been his custom 'since the age of reason' to refuse Communion, and he thought nothing of interrupting a bishop's sermon to say he wanted his breakfast, loudly jangling the coins in his purse.

In recent years efforts have been made to rescue the reputation of a man of whom it was suspected in his lifetime that he had not only murdered his nephew, son of his older brother, Geoffrey, who was the rightful heir to the throne, but had also hanged his wife's admirers from her bedposts.

It was true that John was an ingenious soldier; that, while extracting as much from England as his brother had done, he did not neglect the fleet; that he achieved a reputation amongst the ordinary people of England as a reasonable judge when indulging a taste for the processes of law by hearing cases in his own courts; that he was by no means a

King John hunting stags in one of the royal forests.

philistine, and had a well-chosen selection of books; that he was, for his time, remarkable for his personal cleanliness. But of his covetousness and callous insensitivity there can be no doubt. He treated churchmen with the coarse levity of William II, and extorted all he could by way of feudal dues from the barons while relentlessly pursuing their wives and demanding dowries from their daughters when they wished to marry. Neither lawyers nor merchants, nor knights nor burgesses escaped his depredations; and if the Jews were shielded from such attacks as they had suffered during the enthusiasm aroused by preparations for the Third Crusade, they were protected largely for the benefit of the royal treasury.

Like his father, he provoked a quarrel with the Pope by insisting upon the appointment as Archbishop of Canterbury of one of his advisers, John de Grey, Bishop of Norwich, 'a pleasant and facetious companion', and refusing to approve the consecration of the far more suitable Stephen Langton, a friend and fellow student of the Pope. By way of retaliation, the Pope placed England under an interdict, prohibiting the celebration of Mass; and in 1209 excommunicated the King who professed himself quite unconcerned by the punishment. Four years later, however, when England was threatened by a French invasion supported by the Pope, John was obliged to come to terms with the Papacy and to accept Langton as Archbishop.

It was a capitulation with fateful consequences, for Langton, an Englishman by birth, a cardinal and theological scholar of international repute, made no secret of his sympathy for the barons in their differences with the King and, when certain magnates in the north and east broke out in revolt against royal tyranny and in defence of their customary rights, he acted as mediator and played a leading part in persuading the King that he must come to an agreement with the barons or face the consequences of civil war. Langton also helped to persuade the more extreme barons that they should include with their own demands certain others which might benefit the people as a whole.

The barons' charter, or Magna Carta as it came to be known, was presented by a delegation of their class to the King and his advisers in the early summer of 1215 at a conference at Runnymede, an island in the Thames four miles downstream from Windsor. After the negotiations of the day were over, John returned each evening to the Castle where he is reported to have rolled on the floor in his rage in the characteristic Angevin manner, clawing at the air, gnawing sticks and straw, his face mottled with blue spots. His violent protests were of no avail. In the end, with the utmost reluctance, he was obliged to put his seal to the Charter on 19 June.

The Magna Carta was signed by King John on Runnymede Island near Windsor in 1215.

Previous page:
Effigy of the Black Prince
on his tomb in Canterbury
Cathedral.

Despite the importance subsequently attached to the Magna Carta both in Britain and the United States, the document was less the declaration of human rights it has often been supposed to be than a statement of the feudal and legal relationship between the Crown and the barons, a guarantee of the freedom of the Church and a limitation of the powers of the King. There are, however, clauses which promised more general rights. One in particular proclaimed that 'to none will we sell, to none will we refuse or delay right or justice'; another declared, 'No freeman shall be arrested or imprisoned ... or outlawed or exiled ... except by the lawful judgement of his peers and the laws of the land.' But virtually nothing was said about serfs.

Enraged by his having to sign the Charter, King John immediately denied its validity and, declaring that it had been wrung from him under duress, he prepared to fight the barons, while they, pretending to hold a tournament at Staines, assembled their own army and called upon the King of France to assist them. A French army landed in Kent and marched towards London; and John, ransacking castles and churches and burning crops on the way, withdrew northeast into East Anglia. While his army was crossing the neck of the Wash the tide came in and all his treasures and loot were lost. Distraught by this misfortune he went on disconsolately to the abbey of Swineshead, which had been founded by the Cistercians, an order of monks, an offshoot of the Benedictines, one of the several monastic orders which had established abbeys in England since the foundation of St Augustine's monastery at Canterbury towards the end of the sixth century. Here, after finishing one of his habitually heavy meals with a surfeit of peaches and sweet ale, John contracted dysentery, became feverish and died at Newark on 19 October 1216 at the age of fifty.

Head of King Henry III
from the effigy on his tomb
in Westminster Abbey.

His nine-year-old son and heir, who was taken to Gloucester to be crowned as King Henry III, was then a tractable boy under the tutelage of Hubert de Burgh, the chief justiciar or principal minister in the kingdom, who fulfilled the duties which might roughly be compared to those of a prime minister today. After successfully defending Dover Castle, which he called 'the Key of England', from the French army, Hubert de Burgh won a notable naval victory in the Channel against a far greater number of French ships, whose commander and crews were all slaughtered except for those from whom ransoms might be extracted. Deprived by this defeat of his expected reinforcements, the French King agreed to withdraw from England upon the payment of a large sum of money, giving an undertaking, not fulfilled, to return Normandy to the English Crown. After the withdrawal of the French, order was restored; Stephen Langton, who had left the country in King John's reign, returned to Canterbury; and Hubert de Burgh administered the kingdom in the name of the young King.

As he grew up, however, Henry became more and more disinclined to take the advice of his English advisers, listening rather to his mother, Queen Isabella of Angoulême, to his wife, Eleanor, daughter of the Count of Provence, and to other foreign advisers in whose company he felt more at ease than he did with Englishmen. By the time of Hubert de Burgh's death in 1243, Henry was as much at odds with his barons as his father had been. He had grown into a shiftless and extravagant man, incompetent as a soldier and politician, and incapable of arousing respect or even much affection. He was extremely pious, attending Mass three times a day, taking great pleasure in religious ceremonies and lavishing money upon religious foundations, including Netley Abbey, overlooking Southampton Water, Westminster Abbey which was largely rebuilt in his reign, and the Domus Conversorum, a hostel for converted Jews, monuments from whose chapel are now in the Public Record Office which was built on its site.

For a time one of his particular favourites was Simon de Montfort, a Norman nobleman who had inherited the earldom of Leicester and had married the Queen's sister. Simon soon annoyed the King, however, by pressing for the

The seal of Simon de Montfort, leader of the barons in their quarrel with Henry III.

same reforms as had been urged upon his father, and then exasperated him by presuming, although a Frenchman by birth, not only to become the acknowledged leader of the English barons – who were now meeting together more frequently than they had done in the past to discuss shared problems and affairs of state – but also to advocate the rights of less privileged classes. The King's demands for money to enable his son to be crowned King of Sicily and his brother to become King of the Romans brought matters to a head; and in 1258 it was demanded of Henry that he should appoint a new Great Council of twenty-four members, half of whom were to be nominated by the barons themselves. The members of this Council made their way with their armed retinues to Oxford where they called upon the King to rule with the advice of a smaller Council of fifteen nobles and bishops to be appointed by the recently created Great Council.

Encouraged by his wife and the Pope to defy the barons, Henry claimed that the Provisions of Oxford, which were a clear usurpation of royal power, had been forced upon him under duress. One day that summer, while the King was being rowed down the Thames in London, a storm broke out overhead, obliging him to seek shelter in Durham House, then occupied by Simon de Montfort who came out to greet him at the river steps and to assure him that the storm was over. 'I fear thunder and lightning exceedingly,' the King replied, 'but by God's head, I fear thee more than all the thunder and lightning in the world.'

He had good reason to do so; for when the inevitable civil war broke out between the King's supporters, mostly foreign mercenaries, and the baronial army led by Simon de Montfort, Henry was decisively beaten at Lewes in Sussex in May 1264, despite the routing on the left wing of the citizens of London by the King's son, Edward.

After this battle, while the King and Prince Edward were kept in prison, Simon de Montfort, Edward's godfather, summoned the Great Council to meet at Westminster together with representatives from every shire and nearly all the larger towns, a meeting which has been seen as that of the earliest parliament, a word not then in use in this sense, but one which later came to mean the supreme legislature of the country, comprising the sovereign, the Lords and the Commons assembled in Westminster.

The new constitution, however, was premature. Simon de Montfort's successes, his fiery temper and autocratic manner, the power he now wielded and the excesses of some of his adherents in their attacks upon royalists had made him many enemies. And when Prince Edward escaped from his captors, he was soon able to raise a formidable royal army far larger than that which Simon could bring against it. The two armies met at Evesham in August 1265. 'Let us commend our souls to God,' Simon declared when he saw the size of the enemy host, 'for our bodies are theirs.' So it proved to be. The resultant clash was a massacre rather than a battle; and Simon himself was hacked to pieces, the dismembered parts of his body being despatched for public display in towns which had supported him. Prince Edward, now twenty-six years old, took over the administration of the realm from his father who had been wounded in the shoulder at Evesham, where, held as a hostage on the battlefield, he had not been recognized by his son's men.

Edward was a tall and commanding figure who ate sparingly and drank little but water. He was said to have been capable in his youth of acts of wanton cruelty, once helping his bodyguard to torture and mutilate a peasant whom they had come across on the road. But in recent years, while often merciless in dealing with defeated rebels, he had gained a reputation for courtesy and fair dealing, high intelligence and untiring energy. Devoted to his wife, he was deeply distressed when she died in Nottinghamshire and, having ordered that her body should be brought south to Westminster for burial, he asked that memorial crosses should be erected in all the towns in which the funeral cortège rested on the way. The last of these was put up in

King Edward I, who came to the throne in 1272, with monks and bishops.

75

Effigy of Eleanor of
Castile, wife of Edward I,
on her tomb in
Westminster Abbey.

the small hamlet of Charing, now the busy London area of
Charing Cross where a replica, based on drawings of the
original cross – long since broken up for use as paving
stones and knife handles – was placed in the railway station
forecourt in 1865.

Edward, who had taken the cross on the Eighth Crusade,
was in Sicily when news reached him of his father's death in
1272; but since the realm was reportedly tranquil and in
good hands, he made no haste in his journey home, sending
couriers to England with his instructions and arriving
himself at Dover on 2 August 1274.

Shrewd and painstaking, with an instinctive understanding of political possibilities, Edward presided over the continuing development of Parliament and the reform of the
law, insisting upon the predominance of public over private
jurisdiction, and making it clear that such baronial courts as
still existed only did so by royal consent. He also became
identified with the new spirit of aggressive nationalism,
expelling from the country the Jews – who were already
required to wear a distinguishing badge when walking the
streets and forbidden to employ Christian servants – and
marching at the head of armies intent upon the conquest of
Wales and the subjugation of Scotland.

Northern and western Wales had long resisted penetra-
tion, the Celtic lords jealously retaining their old language
and fostering amongst their people a profound dislike and
distrust of English and Norman alike. The most gifted and
powerful of these leaders, Llewelyn ap Gruffydd, who
called himself Prince of Wales, maintained a long resistance
to Edward's armies, but he was eventually killed in battle
and Welsh independence was lost. To keep control over the
Welsh people, a strong chain of castles was built, from
Caerphilly Castle in the south to Beaumaris and Conway in
the north and Harlech in the west. At one of the largest of
these strongholds, Caernarfon Castle, Edward's heir was
born and in 1301 created Prince of Wales, the title ever
afterwards borne by the male heir to the English throne.

As Llewelyn's opposition had provided Edward with an excuse to subdue Wales, so the refusal of John de Baliol, who had recently become King of Scotland, to accept the overlordship of England gave him an excuse to march against the Scots. His army, thirty-five thousand strong, crossed the Tweed in March 1296 and, with the help of the long bow which Llewelyn's archers had used so effectively against them in Wales, defeated the Scots, took Baliol prisoner and forced him to surrender his crown. Edward returned in triumph to England carrying with him the Stone of Scone on which the Kings of Scotland had long been crowned. He took it to Westminster Abbey where it can still be seen beneath the Coronation Chair which Edward had constructed to enclose it and which has been used for every coronation performed in the Abbey since his time.

The late-13th-century Coronation Chair in Westminster Abbey with the coronation seat of the early Scottish Kings, the Stone of Scone, beneath.

The Scots, however, were not yet subdued. First under Sir William Wallace, who declared himself Guardian of Scotland, and was hanged, drawn and quartered after his defeat, then under Robert Bruce, who was crowned King of Scotland by the Bishop of St Andrew's at Scone, resistance continued long after the death of Edward I who requested in his last hours that his bones should be carried from place to place wherever his army marched against the Scots so that he might, even in death, be said to have led it to victory. He asked also that beside his motto *Pactum Serva*, Keep Faith, there should be inscribed on his tombstone the words *Scotorum Malleus*, the Hammer of the Scots.

Edward's expensive campaigns necessitated his summoning his Council, now more generally known as Parliament, from time to time in order to raise money to pay for them, since the ordinary revenues of the Crown were insufficient for the waging of war and extraordinary taxation could not be levied without parliamentary approval. Concerned to have the votes of rich merchants and of the burgesses of the towns, he saw to it that they were represented at these meetings as well as nobles and prelates. At the Parliament of 1295 – later known as the Model Parliament because it was

A 13th-century master mason supervising stone-cutters in the building of a cathedral.

more representative than any of its predecessors – there were, for instance, among the earls and barons, the arch-bishops, bishops and heads of religious houses, two knights from each shire and two delegates from each city and borough. These men, representing the ordinary citizens of the towns, did not attend with any enthusiasm, knowing that their presence was required merely for financial reasons. Indeed, they had to be coerced by the threat of fines for non-attendance; but gradually they became more and more important as Parliament extended its control over taxation, and eventually sat separately from the nobles and upper clergy in their own chamber, the recently constructed Chapter House of Westminster Abbey, before occupying the chamber that was especially built for them, the House of Commons, sometimes also now known as the Lower House, distinguishing it from the Upper House – the meeting place of the assembly of nobles which still includes bishops as well as peers – the House of Lords.

Despite unrest at home and costly wars abroad, the thir-teenth century was, as a whole, a golden age for building. The Romanesque style had given way to the first phase of Gothic, a word which, as applied pejoratively to a suppos-edly barbarous architectural style, came into use in the sev-enteenth century. This first phase of Gothic became known as Early English, a style characterized by narrow lancet windows terminating in a pointed arch, by circular, or occa-sionally octagonal pillars and by moulded capitals, some-times carved with foliage. It is seen at its most resplendent in Salisbury Cathedral, the west front of Wells Cathedral, the Angel Choir of Lincoln Cathedral – 'out and out,' in Ruskin's words, 'the most precious piece of architecture in the British Isles' – and, more restrainedly, at York Minster where the stained glass is of an unsurpassed beauty.

Nor was it only an age of ecclesiastical building. At Oxford, where a University had been established around the church of St Mary the Virgin, three colleges, University, Balliol and Merton College, had been founded before the end of the thirteenth century and four more, Exeter, Oriel, Queen's and New College, were shortly to follow them. Here Robert Grosseteste, the great Bishop of Lincoln, in whose huge diocese Oxford then lay, was appointed Chancellor in about 1223; and Roger Bacon, the philosopher and one of the foremost experimental scientists of his time, had a study on a tower on Folly Bridge. At Cambridge also a University was established, and St Peter's College or Peterhouse, the oldest of its colleges, was founded by the Bishop of Ely in 1281.

The Chained Library in Hereford Cathedral.

Law was not then taught at either Oxford or Cambridge, where the teaching was largely of grammar, philosophy and theology, the lectures being given in Latin, and this led to the establishment of hostels or inns for students of law in what are still the Inns of Court in London, namely Lincoln's Inn, Gray's Inn, the Middle Temple and the Inner Temple, the names of the last two Inns being derived from the Knights Templar, a brotherhood in arms devoted to the protection of pilgrims in the Holy Land. Their church here, Temple Church, is a fine example of the Transitional style between Romanesque and Early English, a style which can

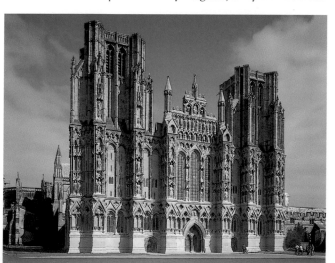

The west front of Wells Cathedral, c.1230-60.

Students of law under instruction.

Edward II with Isabella of France, whom he married in 1308.

also be seen in the nave of Fountains Abbey and the retro-choir of Chichester Cathedral.

While the masons were at work at Chichester, Edward I's son and heir, Edward II, was crowned at Westminster. Ill-educated and indiscreet, Edward II affected the manners of the grooms of his stables whose company he preferred to that of his father's ministers, most of whom he dismissed from office. An excessively heavy drinker, he had a petulant temper and would often strike across the face members of his household who offended him. He was frequently to be found engaged in amateur theatricals when affairs of state awaited his attention or in the company of his intimate friend and presumed lover, Piers Gaveston, the grasping, insolent son of a Gascon knight whom his father had banished but whom he now recalled and created Earl of Cornwall to the fury of the English barons. The barons were not, however, prepared to tolerate Gaveston for long: in 1312 a group of them carried him away a prisoner and cut his head off.

The problem of Scotland could not be settled so expeditiously. Robert Bruce was still at large in command of a formidable army north of the border, capturing one by one the castles still in English hands; and when a large English army, at least three times the size of his own, marched against him he skilfully outmanoeuvred it, trapped it in a bog beside the Bannock Burn on 24 June 1314 and overwhelmed it, sending King Edward, who had remained at the rear with attendant bishops, flying for his life to Dunbar and driving his surviving soldiers after him.

More despised than ever, Edward returned to England where he solaced himself with his new favourites, the Despensers, father and son, men as avaricious and grasping as Gaveston had ever been. The history of the rest of Edward's reign is a tale of blood and betrayal. The barons rose up against the King and the Despensers and were defeated in 1322 at Boroughbridge in Yorkshire where the leader of the baronial party, the Earl of Lancaster, was taken prisoner and later beheaded; Edward's wife left him and took their son to France where the rebel exile, Roger Mortimer, eighth Baron of Wigmore and owner of large estates on the Welsh Marches, became her lover. He and the Queen returned to England in 1326 with a force of mercenaries, soon to be joined by numbers of English supporters of all classes as anxious to see an end to Edward's rule as were the Queen and Mortimer. They defeated the King's forces and forced him to abdicate in favour of his son, now fourteen years old. Both Despensers were forced to suffer a traitor's death; and Edward was imprisoned in Berkeley Castle north of Bristol. Held in a dark cell over a charnel-house, it was hoped he would contract some fatal disease; but surviving this treatment he was murdered, traditionally by having a red-hot spit thrust up his anus into his entrails, an end, so it was said, befitting so shameless a sodomite. His apparently unharmed body, displayed for a time as evidence of his death from natural causes, was taken for burial to the Abbey of St Peter, now Gloucester Cathedral where the effigy upon his tomb beneath a finely carved and many-pinnacled canopy is one of the most beautiful alabaster figures made in the fourteenth century.

The execution of Hugh Despenser, Edward II's favourite, in 1326, from Froissart's *Chronicles* of 1340.

The King's son who ordered the making of this tomb and came to the throne as Edward III in 1327 seemed to be in many ways the very antithesis of his father. Like him he was extravagant, ostentatious and intemperate; but, whereas the father was craven, the son was extravagantly brave; and, while Edward II had been an actor *manqué*, Edward III thought of himself as an Arthurian knight, living in a lost world of romantic chivalry. After a brief foray into Scotland, he turned his attention to France, partly to provide exciting and profitable adventures for those who might otherwise make trouble at home, partly because the Scots were turning increasingly to France for help against the English, and partly to thwart French moves against the cities of Flanders with which the by now extremely prosperous English wool trade was so closely connected.

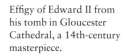

Effigy of Edward II from his tomb in Gloucester Cathedral, a 14th-century masterpiece.

Edward III founded the
Order of the Garter
in 1348.

Claiming the French throne through his mother, Isabella, daughter of Philip IV, he declared a war that was to last for a hundred years. At first he was brilliantly successful: he won a great naval victory at Sluys on 24 June 1340, then an equally decisive land battle near Calais at Crécy where his sixteen-year-old son, soon to be known as the Black Prince because of his unusually dark armour, greatly distinguished himself and, so it is said, by adopting as his own the crest of three feathers and the maxim *'Ich dien'* ('I serve') of the blind King of Bohemia, who had been slain in the opposing army, provided a badge and motto for all future Princes of Wales.

The King went on to take Calais; and in 1356 at Poitiers his son, the Black Prince, won another victory over the French King who was taken prisoner and held to ransom. By the Treaty of Brétigny, Edward III gained much of what he had fought for, absolute control over great territories in the south-west that stretched almost from the Loire to the Pyrenees and, in the north, Calais and Ponthieu.

The English defeat the
French in the battle
of Crécy in 1346.

After his earlier victories Edward III had returned home in triumph with wagonloads of plunder, clothes and furs, feather beds and the spoils of foreign cities. It was said that 'all England was filled with the spoils of the King's expedition, so that there was not a woman who did not wear some ornament, or have in her house fine linen or some goblet, part of the booty' brought home.

Yet the wild extravagance of the victors' celebrations seemed to some chroniclers wickedly wanton, in particular the merriment at Windsor whence there came reports of the most prodigal festivities, of 'feasts complete with richness of fare, variety of dishes, and overflowing abundance of drinks'. In the Upper Ward of the Castle, the King ordered the construction of a magnificent circular stone feasting hall in which would be held the meetings of the knights of a new 'Round Table in the same manner and conditions as the Lord Arthur, formerly King of England, appointed it'. These knights were to be bound together by 'a badge of unity and concord', a garter. The story went – and recent research has indicated that it may well be true – that the King was dancing at a ball in the Castle with Joan, Countess of Salisbury, when her garter fell off. Edward stooped and picked it up. Some of the other dancers saw him do so and began to tease him. He replied sharply, speaking in French which was the language he used in ordinary conversation – though he is believed to be the first King of England after the Conquest, with the possible exception of Henry I, to have been able to speak English – '*Honi soit qui mal y pense*' ('shame on him who thinks ill of it'), thus providing the motto of the oldest extant order of knighthood in Europe.

This was in 1348, a year in which the festivities at Windsor seemed all the more reprehensible to the chroniclers, for it was the dreadful year in which 'the cruel pestilence, terrible to all future ages, came from parts over the sea to the south coast of England, into a port called Melcombe in Dorsetshire'. This plague or Great Mortality,

Edward III with his son, the Black Prince.

The Star, part of the regalia of the Order of the Garter.

83

much later to be known as the Black Death, 'passed most rapidly from place to place,' recorded the Registrar of the Court of Canterbury, 'swiftly killing ere mid-day many who in the morning had been well, and without respect of persons'. The first symptoms were swellings in various parts of the body, particularly in the groin and under the arms, then the eruption of black pustules. Delirium soon followed, and the vomiting of blood. Few who were infected escaped death, and that within a few hours. When the summer of 1348 gave way to colder weather the spread of the plague was halted for a time but when spring came it renewed its course more virulently than ever. The towns were the worst affected places; but small villages did not escape and in some the inhabitants were entirely wiped out. Only the remote areas of the north-west, the mountainous regions of Wales and Scotland and west Cornwall, remained immune.

It has been estimated that almost half the people in the country perished. It does, indeed, seem likely that the population, which had risen to about 4,250,000 by 1300, had fallen to about 2,500,000 by 1380. The Black Death was not entirely responsible for this sharp fall: there were other outbreaks of plague and occasional famine, while sheep farming, which required a relatively small labour force, was extending over large areas at the expense of corn growing.

In the plague of 1348, later known as the Black Death, probably as many as half the population of England died.

But the Black Death, a fearful visitation which contributed much to the macabre nature of later medieval literature, was undoubtedly the main cause of the dramatic fall in population and of the acceleration of far-reaching changes already noticeable in English society.

The sharp decline in the population of England naturally resulted in an acute labour shortage as well as a plentiful supply of land for the surviving peasants. Many peasants were able to increase their holdings by taking over the fields of those who had died; others, who had no land, were able to demand greater rewards for their services and went off to other manors if they did not get them. The King, preoccupied with his foreign wars and, in his premature senility, with his rapacious mistress, Alice Perrers, allowed the government to fall into the hands of his fourth son, John of Gaunt, Duke of Lancaster, who was thought to be intent on gaining a controlling influence over the King's grandson, later Richard II, or even to be contriving to gain the crown for himself. In an effort to overcome their financial and social problems the government in 1351 issued a Statute of Labourers which made it a crime for peasants to ask for more wages or for their employers to pay more than the rates laid down by the Justices of the Peace, the local gentry with judicial powers to try cases relating to public order in the counties, the ancestors of the present Justices who still have power to try lesser cases, committing the more serious to a higher court. A later Statute proposed that any labourer who left his place of work to seek higher wages should be branded with the letter F on his forehead as a sign of falsehood. It soon even became a crime for a labourer to dress as though he were a landlord and for 'common lewd women' to dress like 'good noble dames'.

Such repressive measures, combined with the imposition of a series of taxes known as poll taxes and levied on everyone over fifteen, caused deep and widespread discontent which was exacerbated by resentment against the riches and corruption of the higher clergy. John Wyclif, for a time

A peasant harvesting, in the years following the Black Death.

Richard II, the Black Prince's son, who came to the throne in 1377.

A bailiff with stick and hunting horn berates his master's labourers.

Master of Balliol College, Oxford, spoke for thousands when he urged the disendowment of the Church and a return to evangelical poverty; and his 'poor priests', known as Lollards – a word meaning mumbler of prayers applied to them derisively by William Courtenay, Archbishop of Canterbury – went about the country preaching Wyclif's doctrines and condemning the ecclesiastical hierarchy and the material possessions of the Church. Speaking more bluntly and, on occasions, crudely, John Ball, an eloquent and fiery excommunicated priest, marched from market place to churchyard, castigating the ways of the clergy and preaching upon the contentious text:

> When Adam dalf [dug] and Eve span
> Who was thanne a gentilman?

Soon whole districts were in uproar. Manors and religious houses were attacked; lords and priors murdered; and the cry went up, 'Death to all lawyers. John Ball hath rungeth your bell!'

Led by one Walter, a man supposed to have been either an ex-soldier or a highwayman but generally known as Wat Tyler because of his trade, the men of Kent and Essex, forming bands of armed villagers and townsmen, descended on London in June 1381, releasing John Ball from Maidstone gaol on the way. They poured into Southwark; ransacked Lambeth Palace, the Archbishop of Canterbury's house since the end of the twelfth century; crossed London Bridge between the houses which had been built on it from bank to bank; marched down Fleet Street; burst into the Temple where they burned the lawyers' rolls; opened the gates of the Fleet prison; attacked the houses of foreign merchants; and, 'like packs of hungry wolves', made their way to Savoy Palace, the great mansion in the Strand which had been granted by Henry III to his wife's uncle, the Count of Savoy, and was now occupied by the King's hated uncle, John of Gaunt.

The Duke escaped but his doctor and sergeant-at-arms were both killed; the palace was ransacked and set alight; the explosion of a box of gunpowder consigned to the flames brought down the Great Hall; and thirty-two men who were drinking the Duke's wine were trapped when the cellar ceiling collapsed on them.

The mob, 'howling like men possessed', now turned their attention to the Tower. Forcing their way across the drawbridges and through the gates, they dashed through the Great Hall and the Wardrobe into the private apartments of the King's mother where they tore down her hangings and

The Lord Mayor of London strikes down Wat Tyler in the presence of the 14-year-old Richard II in the Peasants' Revolt of 1381.

cut her bedclothes into ribbons. She herself escaped in the confusion; but, in the Chapel of St John, the rebels came upon the Lord Treasurer and the Archbishop of Canterbury praying before the altar. They dragged them out and, with other victims, beheaded them on Tower Hill, parading their heads about the city on spikes. Meanwhile, another rebel leader, Jack Straw, led his men north to attack the Treasurer's house at Highbury and to burn down the Priory of St John, Clerkenwell.

The next day, 15 June, the fourteen-year-old King Richard met the rebels at Smithfield in an open field where horse sales were held, and there he acceded to most of their requests. Yet Tyler's arrogant disrespect so enraged the Lord Mayor, William Walworth, a fishmonger, that he lashed out at the man with the flat of his sword, knocking him off his horse to the ground where he was stabbed to death with a dagger which is displayed, with various treasures of the Fishmongers' Company, in Fishmongers' Hall, King William Street. Brandishing their weapons, the rebels advanced upon the King's retinue. But Richard rode towards them, calling out, 'Sirs, will you kill your King? I am your captain. Follow me.' Responding to this plea, they rode away with him towards Clerkenwell where they dispersed, trusting him to keep the promises he had made to them. But these were all broken on the grounds that they had been obtained under duress; and, when reminded of his undertakings to abolish feudal services, the King is said to have riposted, 'Villeins you are, and villeins you will remain.' Although the poll tax was abandoned, the survivors of the revolt returned to their homes to resume their seemingly immutable lives.

THE STRUGGLE FOR POWER

From the suppression of the Peasants' Revolt (1381)
to the restoration (1660)

A fireside scene from the Bedford Hours, c. 1423.

Previous page:
Knights jousting, from a 15th-century treatise on heraldry.

The cloisters of Gloucester Cathedral, completed in 1412.

Although the wearisome daily round of a farm labourer changed little during the fourteenth century, society was slowly being transformed nevertheless, and there was beginning to be discerned a gradual shift in the balance of power. Not only were industrious peasants increasing their holdings in the aftermath of the Black Death; not only were those who had no holdings successfully pressing for higher rewards for their labour; but landlords were being obliged by the labour shortage to let land either for money rent or for payment in kind, while many of their tenants were becoming quite prosperous yeomen farmers whose interests were more closely identified with those of the lesser gentry than with those of landless labourers. The Pastons, for example, the well-to-do Norfolk family whose correspondence provides so illuminating a picture of late medieval domestic life, had but lately risen from the lowly estate of husbandmen bound to the land for life.

The landscape in which these people spent their lives had been changing for some time, too. The years immediately before the Black Death had been an era of economic decline: large areas of land had fallen out of agricultural use; water had poured back over acre upon acre of drained fenland; and the foundation of new towns came almost to an end. The Black Death had much accelerated this depression and it was to be many years before the process was reversed. Indeed, the decline in arable farming continued long into the next century as the demand for wool and its price increased and ship after ship sailed with exports to the Continent. To create more land for sheep, arable fields were made into pasture; and whole villages were destroyed and their inhabitants evicted to make way for new flocks. At the same time the fortunes being made by wool farmers and wool merchants were being used to create the buildings which are still so distinctive a feature of the English scene. In nearly every English county, by wealthy tinners in Devon and Cornwall, as well as by individuals and communities doing so well in the wool trade, churches were being built and reconstructed

94

in the style known as Perpendicular, the last stage of Gothic, a style distinguished by large windows with a predominance of vertical lines in their stone tracery and regular horizontal divisions, and by the kind of fan vaulting to be seen in the cloisters of Gloucester Cathedral. Beautiful examples of Perpendicular churches can be seen, for example, in Wiltshire at Steeple Aston, in Somerset at Huish Episcopi, in Norfolk at Salle, in Gloucestershire at Cirencester; in Suffolk at Long Melford as well as at Lavenham where, indeed, the whole town is a monument to the prosperity of the wool and clothing trade of the late Middle Ages.

Medieval houses in Lavenham, Suffolk.

In Kent, too, and in the north-west Midlands are numerous examples of the comfortable houses being built by merchants and yeomen farmers whose wealth, if not power, was beginning to rival that of the old ruling class. Castles were still being built as well as houses, several of them brick like Tattershall Castle in Lincolnshire and Herstmonceux in Sussex; and these, with more doors and many more windows, were becoming – while still formidable enough in appearance – more like homes than fortresses, since the increasing use of gunpowder and the power of cannon had rendered the most sturdy defences vulnerable to assault.

Geoffrey Chaucer, from an illustration in Hoccleve's *De Regimine Principum*, published shortly after his death in 1400.

Bricks were not a new building material. Imported from the Continent and known as Flanders tiles, they had been used since the beginning of the thirteenth century when Little Wenham Hall had been built on the borders of Suffolk and Essex. This, however, was an unusual example until the brick buildings of France attracted the attention of knights fighting there. The English word 'brick' from the French '*brique*' did not even enter the language until 1416; and the town wall at Kingston Upon Hull, built in the second half of the fourteenth century of locally-made bricks, was probably the first major public work to be constructed in England of this material. Thereafter brick became much more commonly used even in districts where the local material was stone, as at Compton Wynyates in Warwickshire. Two and a half million bricks were used in the building of Eton

Compton Wynyates, the Marquess of Northampton's early Tudor house in Warwickshire.

College in the ten years after its foundation in 1440.

The heyday of brick had not yet come, however. Most houses were still of timber or stone. So were most late medieval bridges, several of which still survive, notable examples in stone being those over the Camel at Wadebridge in Cornwall and over the Thames at Abingdon in Oxfordshire. Also, of course, of stone were the finest masterpieces of the Perpendicular style, such as the West Front of Beverley Minster, Eton College Chapel and the Chapel of St George at Windsor, which was dedicated to the obscure third- or fourth-century martyr who, for reasons unexplained, had become England's patron saint. This chapel was begun in 1478 by Edward IV, determined to outdo Eton College Chapel, the nearby foundation of his rival and victim, Henry VI.

Henry VI's grandfather, the eldest surviving son of John of Gaunt, Duke of Lancaster, and known as Henry Bolingbroke after the Lincolnshire Castle where he was born, had supplanted his cousin, Richard II, in 1399 and had become the first of the Lancastrian kings. In Westminster Hall – the splendid Norman banqueting hall built by William II which is the only surviving part of the original Palace of Westminster – Henry had called out in English, long since the lan-

Henry Bolingbroke, who became King Henry IV in 1399, entering London.

Illustration in a
15th-century manuscript
showing Parliament
proclaiming the Duke
of Lancaster as Henry IV
in 1399.

guage not only of ordinary people but also of the law courts,
'In the name of Fadir Son and Holy Ghost, I Henry of
Lancaster chalenge this Rewme of Ingland and the Corone.'
The Archbishops of York and Canterbury had led him to the
throne vacated by the deposed Richard II and, soon after-
wards, he had been anointed with the oil which the Virgin
Mary had miraculously given to St Thomas in his exile.

Yet while accepted by Parliament, Henry IV was no more
able to come to satisfactory terms with its members than his
predecessor had been. Beset by financial and administrative
problems, by conspirators in his own country and by rebels
in Wales, he fell ill in 1412 with what the chroniclers
described as leprosy but may well have been syphilis with
which leprosy was then often confused. He died in the
Jerusalem Chamber at Westminster Abbey, where he had
been praying before St Edward's shrine, and was buried in
Canterbury Cathedral, where his magnificent tomb lies
behind the high altar.

His son, Henry V, who was crowned in a violent snow-
storm in April 1413, was every inch a soldier. The back of
his neck and the sides of his head were shaved, as the heads
of soldiers were, so that his hair, thick, brown and uncurled,
looked like a round fur cap. He was considered a handsome

Henry V, Henry IV's son,
the pious soldier.

man, though the long and prominent nose, the thin eyebrows, the high smooth brow, the very red and tightly compressed lips and the heavy lantern jaw are features no longer admired. His energy was legendary and men looking at him found grounds for hope that his father's reign, which had opened with usurpation, rebellion, plague and persecution and had ended in fear, lassitude and gloom, would be followed by a new age, as brilliant and adventurous as that of the young King's great-grandfather, Edward III.

Henry was certainly as anxious to fulfil that dream as he was to engage in some foreign adventure which would distract the attention of his enemies from problems at home and from his far from indisputable title to the English throne. Reviving the claims of his ancestors, he required the return of territories that had been granted to Edward III by the Treaty of Brétigny and later demanded the French crown by right of succession from his great-great-grandmother, Isabella, daughter of Philip IV. And at Agincourt on St Crispin's Day 1415, in an astonishing pitched battle which lasted barely three hours, his depleted, exhausted and hungry army routed a French force four or five times its size, losing no more than a hundred men to the enemy's seven to ten thousand dead. After this extraordinary

The English army of Henry V overwhelms the French at Agincourt, 1415.

victory, Henry was able to impose humiliating terms upon the French King whose daughter he married and whose heir he became. The leadership of all Christendom was now within his grasp and his thoughts turned to a new crusade against the Infidel. But his health broke down in the summer of 1422 and at the age of thirty-five he died at Vincennes. His body was embalmed and brought home to England to be interred in Westminster Abbey in a resplendent tomb beneath the Chantry of Henry V.

Henry V agrees to the Treaty of Troyes with the French King, 1420.

He left England in the care of a regent and a baby king who eventually, having neither his powers of leadership nor his degree of parliamentary support and having to contend with the rising force of French national pride and its inspired epitome, Joan of Arc, was to lose all that his father had fought for by the time the Hundred Years' War ended in 1453.

Henry VI, who was only eight months old at the time of his accession, was to lose more than France. A kind, simple-minded man more interested in his religious observances and benefactions than in government, he lost his reason in 1453 and his life in 1471 when, a prisoner in the Tower, he was found dead in his cell, having passed away, so it was announced, out of 'pure displeasure and melancholy'.

During the last years of his unhappy reign, his supporters had been fighting other claimants to the throne in the dynastic conflict known as the Wars of the Roses. The Lancastrians – represented by Henry VI and led by Henry's Queen Margaret and the descendants of John of Gaunt by his mistress, later wife, Catherine Swynford – were the faction of the red rose, one of the several emblems of their house. Their opponents, the Yorkists – led by Richard, Duke of York, a descendant of Edward III, and by Richard Neville, Earl of Warwick, the most powerful noble in the realm, known as 'The Kingmaker' – bore the white rose. Intermittently, for thirty years, these two factions quarrelled and fought, causing havoc in the areas where they clashed, yet, when their armies had passed by, leaving the

Henry VI, founder of Eton College and King's College, Cambridge, reigned 1422-61, and 1470-1.

The Yorkists rout the Lancastrians at Tewkesbury in the Wars of the Roses, 1471.

merchants and the great mass of the people to carry on with their work as in times of perfect tranquillity. At length the Duke of York's son, Edward, emerged the victor, after deposing King Henry VI in 1461 and inflicting a series of defeats on the Lancastrians, culminating in their rout in 1471 at Tewkesbury.

With nearly all his leading opponents either killed in the battle or executed afterwards, Edward's position was now secure; and as King Edward IV he set about restoring the finances of the Crown and the disrupted export trade of the country. Virtually dispensing with Parliament, so many of whose members had been killed in the recent wars, he raised money by all the other means open to him, taking care to ensure that all the revenues to which the Crown was entitled were collected and administered with the utmost efficiency.

Grateful to him for restoring order to the country and helping to give it a large measure of prosperity, the citizens of London regarded Edward as 'the most noble of kings'. So did their wives, one of whom, Jane Shore, whose husband was a Lombard Street goldsmith, became the most celebrated of Edward's countless mistresses, giving her name to some of London's most squalid eighteenth-century brothels. Over six foot three inches tall, handsome, autocratic and wonderfully energetic, Edward IV was a man of insinuating charm and friendly *bonhomie*. His subjects were prepared to forgive him much; and it was not until the end of his life that his debaucheries and increasingly unscrupulous conduct turned them against him.

He died in 1483 and his thirteen-year-old son was proclaimed his successor as Edward V. While awaiting his coronation the new King and his younger brother were lodged in the Tower; and it was announced that for the time being their uncle, Edward IV's brother, Richard, Duke of Gloucester, had been appointed to the office of Protector.

To some historians, Richard of Gloucester remains the monster that William Shakespeare portrayed. To others, discrediting the propaganda of those who defeated him,

Richard III, the last of the Plantagenet Kings, killed at Bosworth Field, 1485.

he is a paragon. Undoubtedly he was not the sanguinary hunchback of popular imagination; nor was he guilty of many of the atrocious crimes attributed to him. Yet he was not a man whose character was out of tune with the ruthless spirit of his times; and, although there is no reliable evidence that he was responsible for the murders of Edward V and his brother, who never emerged from the Tower, there is also no evidence that he was not.

Whether responsible for the crime or not, he did not live to profit from it long. For on 22 August 1485 at Bosworth Field in Leicestershire, in the last battle of the Wars of the Roses, he lost his crown and his life to yet another claimant to the throne, Henry Tudor, the son of a Welsh knight, whose mother was a great-granddaughter of John of Gaunt. Soon after his victory, Henry Tudor married Edward IV's daughter, Elizabeth, thus uniting the Houses of Lancaster and York, a reconciliation symbolized by the red and white rose of the House of Tudor.

The fifteenth century was now drawing to a close. It was a century described by the Victorian historian, Bishop William Stubbs, as 'futile, bloody and immoral' and by a historian of our own day as the background to a society 'violent, dirty and overdressed.' But it was also the age of John Lydgate's *Troy Book* and of Sir Thomas Malory's *Le Morte d'Arthur*; of Reginald Ely, the Norfolk mason, who built the first court of Queen's College, Cambridge as well as the Chapel of King's College; of Henry Chichele, the Archbishop of Canterbury, who founded All Souls College, Oxford; and of John Glasier who provided the College with some of its beautiful painted glass; of the carvers of William of Wykeham's Chantry in Winchester Cathedral and of the monument in St Albans Cathedral to Henry V's brother, Humfrey, Duke of Gloucester, who presented his large collection of manuscripts to the Bodleian Library, Oxford where the splendid room in which they were housed still bears his name.

A 15th-century shield decorated with a picture of a knight and his lady.

Elizabeth of York, wife of
Henry VII and mother of
Henry VIII.

Previous page:
The Spanish Armada
under attack during its
passage up the Channel
in 1588.

According to a tradition preserved by Shakespeare, when Henry Tudor was brought to London as a boy to be presented to Henry VI, the King, struck by the intelligence of his looks, declared, 'Lo, surely, this is he to whom both we and our adversaries shall hereafter give place.'

Several portraits of Henry VII, as well as the bust of him by Pietro Torrigiani, now in the Victoria and Albert Museum, do, indeed, present the impression of a remarkable man, astute and wary, calculating but not without mercy, grave yet responsive to humour. He was clearly a ruler as capable as any of restoring order to a stricken country, of bringing solvency and honour to the Crown, and of continuing the work begun by his Plantagenet and Lancastrian predecessors. He chose his servants well, esteeming capacity above high birth, ensuring that his financial and judicial agents lost no opportunity of gathering in every penny due to the King who personally supervised their accounts, straining to obtain all that could be gleaned from royal lands and the administration of royal justice, allowing the commissioners of his minister, Richard Foxe, Bishop of Winchester, and of his Lord Chancellor, John Morton, Archbishop of Canterbury, to raise money by the method which became known as Morton's Fork, a form of assessment that extracted money both from those who lived frugally, on the grounds that they must have savings, and from those who lived in grand style, on the grounds that they must be rich. Morton, Foxe and the King's other principal advisers, about half of them bishops, were members of his Privy Council, now effectively the government of the country, the Great Council being in process of development into the House of Lords.

The Lords had been much weakened and reduced by the recent wars – several noble families having been completely wiped out and not replaced by the creation of new peerages – while the Commons – comprising for the most part knights elected by their shires and burgesses from the towns – were summoned only when their assent was needed for the passing of new laws or the raising of taxes. The Privy Council was, therefore, under the King supreme; and its powerful judicial body, the Court of Star Chamber – so known because of the decoration of the ceiling in the room where it met in Whitehall Palace – made its rulings unhampered by the Common Law which was administered by the unpaid Justices of Peace in the country at large. The Council of the North was held responsible for the administration of the northern counties – in so far as these still largely wild regions could be said to be susceptible to royal rule at all – but, in matters of concern to the nation as a whole, the Privy Council had to be consulted.

The accession of the Tudor dynasty in 1485 did not, of course, immediately put an end to strife and rebellion. The impostor, Lambert Simnel, the son of a pastrycook, claiming to be the nephew of Edward IV and crowned in Dublin as King Edward VI, mustered sufficient support for an invasion of England in 1487; but he was soon defeated, and his survival as a scullion in the royal kitchens, and later as a falconer, shows how confident of his safety the King had already become in a country weary of conflict and only too ready to accept autocracy for the sake of peace. Another impostor, Perkin Warbeck, claiming to be the younger of the two princes held in the Tower in the reign of Richard III, also invaded England; but he, too, was soon forced to submit to the King's troops.

Nor did the accession of the Tudors and the ending of the Wars of the Roses bring the Middle Ages to a convenient close. Most people in the country, living and working in their age-old ways, were unaware that any notable change had taken place. A Statute of the second year of the King's reign which referred to him as 'the Sovereign Lord of this land for the time being' might well have seemed well phrased to them, had they ever heard of it. Yet profound changes were, nevertheless, taking place. The ideas of the Renaissance, that flowering of art, literature and politics under the influence of Greek and Roman models, which had

William Caxton, the first English printer, with his trademark and initials.

begun in northern Italy in the previous century or earlier, was now spreading across Europe and inducing men and women to regard themselves and their lives in relation to the world in which they lived rather than to the superhuman world of the old-fashioned theologians and schoolmen. This was the age of John Colet, Dean of St Paul's Cathedral and founder of St Paul's School, who returned to England from Italy in 1496, and of Desiderius Erasmus who came to Oxford from Paris two years later, as well as of William Caxton whose press at Westminster was busily printing the books which were to disseminate the new ideas of their time.

Also, the world was expanding: Portuguese explorers were voyaging ever further south down the coast of Africa; and in 1497 Vasco da Gama made his momentous journey round the Cape of Good Hope to India. Five years earlier, the Genoese, Christopher Columbus, having failed to persuade the English and Portuguese Kings to invest in his enterprise, had sailed across the Atlantic and planted the Spanish flag upon the shores of the New World, claiming it for his sponsors, Ferdinand and Isabella of Spain.

For centuries England had been regarded as an offshore island of relatively small concern in the affairs of western Europe. She was now becoming a nation and a market of importance not only to the Low Countries and the states of the Baltic but also to France and Spain. She was being recognized as a country of expert seamen and experienced merchants, a country whose resources, as yet scarcely known, would one day make her powerful, a country occupying a position which might have been especially designed to enable her to take advantage of the opportunities of trade which the discoveries of the century's explorers now offered Europe. While the marriage of Henry VII's daughter, Margaret, to King James IV of Scotland might have been seen merely as a prudent means of keeping the peace by the union of dynasties – like Henry's own marriage to Elizabeth of York – the match between Henry's son, Prince Arthur, and Catherine of Aragon, daughter of the Spanish King Ferdinand, could not but be interpreted as a sign of England's rising reputation in the eyes of the world.

When Henry VII died in 1509 at fifty-two, an age greater than that reached by any of his four immediate predecessors, he left his son and heir an immense fortune, even though he had not denied himself the pleasures of building. He had lavished immense sums of money upon Henry VII's Chapel in Westminster Abbey – a superb example of the late Perpendicular or Tudor Gothic style – had contributed towards the cost of several institutions established by his mother, Lady Margaret Beaufort, foundress of St John's College and Christ's College, Cambridge, and had spent enormous sums upon the navy whose flagship, the *Mary Rose*, which sank off Portsmouth in 1545, was recently raised and can now be seen in the naval base at Portsmouth.

Henry VII, the first of the Tudor monarchs.

The King's eldest son, Prince Arthur, fourteen years old at the time of his marriage to Catherine of Aragon, had died at Ludlow Castle soon after the wedding. He boasted coarsely that he had been 'six miles into Spain'; but his bride maintained that she was still a virgin at his death. The Pope was accordingly persuaded to grant a dispensation so that she could marry his younger brother, Henry, who had by then become King of England.

Henry VIII was an attractive young man of high intelligence, numerous accomplishments and boundless self-confidence, enjoying to the full both the sports and pastimes of the royal parks and palaces and the intellectual pleasures of a court which was graced, or soon to be graced, by Sir Thomas More, the humanist scholar and statesman and author of *Utopia*, the poets Skelton, Surrey and Wyatt, and the painter Hans Holbein whose portraits and whose followers' portraits of the magnificent King were to adorn the country houses of numerous of his awed and faithful subjects.

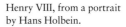

Henry VIII, from a portrait by Hans Holbein.

The King pursued his pleasures and interests with a seemingly tireless energy; but to work he brought little of the

Sir Thomas More, who was executed in 1535, with his father, household and descendants.

Henry VIII's chief minister, Cardinal Thomas Wolsey.

application of his father, content to leave much of the Crown's business in the highly capable and grasping hands of Thomas Wolsey. The son of an Ipswich butcher, Wolsey was immensely rich and powerful, a Cardinal, Archbishop of York as well as Lord Chancellor. His portly figure, clad in sumptuous scarlet and mounted upon a mule – a sponge soaked in vinegar and encased in the peel of an orange held to his nose to keep off the smell of the surrounding throng – could often be seen riding from his splendid palace to Westminster Hall, attended by numerous liveried servants crying out, 'Make way for my Lord's Grace!' It was natural that the King should turn to Wolsey when, tired of Catherine of Aragon, who had given him a daughter but no living son – and obsessively worried by the biblical text: 'And if a man shall take his brother's wife, it is an unclean thing ... They shall be childless' – he set his mind upon a divorce. With this end in view, Wolsey approached the Pope; but the Pope was Clement VII who had recently been driven from Rome by Queen Catherine's uncle, the Emperor Charles V. An indecisive man, distracted by his recent misfortunes, Clement delayed giving the answer which Wolsey and the King required. Henry was by now in love with one of his Queen's ladies, the pert, excitable and sensual Anne Boleyn, great-granddaughter of Sir Geoffrey Boleyn, hatter, mercer and Lord Mayor of London who had bought Blickling Hall in Norfolk and had created of himself a country gentleman. The longer he was obliged to wait, the more determined the King became to make Anne Boleyn his Queen and the mother of his longed-for heir. By the end of 1532, soon after Wolsey's disgrace and death, Anne was known to be bearing Henry's child; and in January the next year they were married, secretly and in haste. Soon afterwards Thomas Cranmer, a married man of reformist views, was confirmed as Archbishop of Canterbury in succession to Queen Catherine's friend, William Warham; and, in early May, an ecclesiastical court convened by Cranmer decreed that the King's marriage to Catherine of Aragon was null and void.

Catherine of Aragon, Henry VIII's first wife, mother of Queen Mary.

The Pope responded by excommunicating the King, while the King initiated the long process of legislation establishing the principle, which several of his predecessors had endeavoured to maintain, that the authority of the King of England was independent of Rome and putting a stop to the revenues that customarily flowed from England into the capacious coffers of the Curia.

To support him in his endeavours to reform the relationship between the King and the Papacy without disturbing Roman Catholic doctrine – or the right of the King to the title Defender of the Faith which had been granted to him by Leo X for a pamphlet he had written on the errors of Protestantism and which in the abbreviated Latin form of Fid Def or FD is still seen on coins of the realm – the King summoned Parliament which his father had called upon only six times in twenty-three years. Parliament obligingly passed the Act of Supremacy which declared the King to be Supreme Head of the Church of England.

Anne Boleyn, Queen Elizabeth I's mother, who was married to Henry VIII in 1533.

The legislation of the Reformation, that religious upheaval which turned Roman Catholic England into a constitutionally Protestant country, was not unpopular with the people at large; nor was the Dissolution of the

109

Title page of the Great
Bible of 1539.

Thomas Cromwell,
Henry VIII's instrument in
the separation of the
English Church from
Rome and the Dissolution
of the Monasteries.

Monasteries which accompanied it. For years anti-clerical feeling had been growing in England and had been exemplified by the satisfaction caused by the fall of Cardinal Wolsey, that archetypal churchman, proud and pompous, who had amassed such immense riches from lay and ecclesiastical offices of profit. For years, too, there had been a growing feeling in the country that most monasteries were fulfilling few if any of the functions for which they had been founded in the Middle Ages, that some of them – in the words of the official pronouncement decreeing inspection of the smaller foundations – were nests of 'manifest sin, vicious, carnal and abominable living'.

Objections were raised to the destruction of the monasteries in certain areas where they were still providing food and shelter for the destitute and travellers, as well as education for the sons of families in the surrounding parishes. In the troublesome north the uprisings known as the Pilgrimage of Grace caused the government disquiet for a time; but in the country generally the Dissolution caused little dismay, however disliked may have been the man employed to carry through the King's revolution, Wolsey's former secretary, Thomas Cromwell, son of a blacksmith who kept a public house at Putney, a man of extraordinary administrative ability and single-minded determination.

As the King's Vicar-General, Cromwell supervised the dismantling of the abbeys, the transfer of their properties and lands to the Crown, and their sale, through the Court of Augmentations, to the English gentry, rich speculators and, most commonly of all, to existing local landowners. Some of England's great abbeys still lie in romantic ruin, among them the Yorkshire abbeys of Kirstall, Jervaulx, Rievaulx and Fountains whose grounds have now been joined to those of Studley Royal. Many others were converted into private houses like Lacock Abbey in Wiltshire and Mottisfont in Hampshire. Several new houses were built in the grounds of dissolved monasteries, like Longleat, Sir John Thynne's mansion on the land of the priory of St

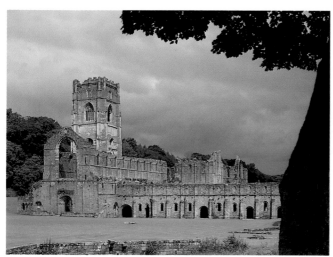

Fountains Abbey in Yorkshire, one of the numerous religious houses to be dissolved in the reign of Henry VIII.

Radegund. The money from very few was used for the endowment of charitable and educational establishments, as the reforming clergy had hoped, though Trinity College, Cambridge was founded by the King in 1546, not long after Christ Church, originally Cardinal's College, had been founded by Wolsey at Oxford following the demolition of the Augustinian St Frideswide's Priory.

By the time most of the abbeys had been transferred to their new owners in 1541, Henry VIII was fifty years old. The handsome, lithe young man had become grossly fat; his fair features had coarsened; he inspired more fear than admiration. Anne Boleyn, increasingly petulant and hysterical, had been beheaded, condemned to death on charges of adultery with several men, including her brother; the King's third wife, Jane Seymour, had died in childbirth, having given him his longed-for son, Edward; the arrival in England of his fourth wife, the excessively plain Anne of Cleves, pressed upon him by Cromwell in pursuit of a German alliance, had led to Cromwell's following to the block the more agreeable figure of Sir Thomas More, executed for refusing to deny the principle of papal supremacy. The King's fifth wife, Catherine Howard, accused of being

Jane Seymour, Henry VIII's third wife, the mother of his heir Edward VI.

111

Catherine Parr,
Henry VIII's sixth wife,
who survived him,
dying in 1548.

as unfaithful to him as Anne Boleyn was alleged to have
been, was beheaded too. At last he found some comfort in
the pain of his declining years in the company of his sixth
wife, Catherine Parr, a good-natured, virtuous widow, who
was kind to his children and sat with his ulcerated leg on her
knee, discussing with him those recondite religious problems which had never failed to interest him.

For most of his reign, Henry VIII punished religious dissidents, whether Roman Catholic or Protestant, with impar-
tiality. His son, Edward VI, however, the cold and 'lonely,
clever boy' who succeeded him at the age of nine, was a convinced Protestant, surrounded by Protestant advisers,
notably his uncle, Edward Seymour, Duke of Somerset,
who had obtained for himself the 'name and title of
Protector of all the Realms and Domains of the King's
Majesty, and Governor of His Most Royal Person'. The
King was still Defender of the Faith but that faith was now
to be ever more avowedly Protestant, as defined by the 42
Articles which formed the basis of the 39 Articles, the cor-
nerstone of the religious settlement of 1563 and still in
force. Hugh Latimer, who had resigned the bishopric of
Worcester in Henry's reign – after preaching forceful

A painting of 1549
depicting Edward VI
and the Pope stunned
by a Bible.

sermons urging on the Reformation which had brought him a prisoner to the Tower – returned to the pulpit to express views more advanced than ever. Thomas Cranmer, Archbishop of Canterbury, who had by now given up his belief in transubstantiation, issued *The Booke of the Common Prayer and Administration of the Sacraments*, the use of which the Act of Uniformity of 1549 required in churches instead of the old Latin services. There being no abbeys left to plunder, the King's advisers turned upon chantries – shrines devoted to prayers for the dead – and seized their endowments. The Duke of Somerset himself lavished a large share of his accumulated riches upon the building of his huge palace, Somerset House in the Strand. To make way for this the Church of the Nativity of Our Lady and the Innocents was demolished and, to provide the stone for it, much of the Priory Church of St John Clerkenwell was blown up, little of the building being spared, apart from the south gate, St John's Gate. Attempts were made to take stone also from St Margaret's West-minster but the parishioners here drove the Duke's men off.

Elsewhere in the country, there were protests not only against the imposition of religious changes but also against the continuing revolution in agriculture: in Devon and Cornwall people rebelled against having to use a prayer book rather than the Latin forms with which they had been so long familiar; and in East Anglia in 1547 there was a rebellion, led by Robert Kett, a well-to-do landowner, against the growing practices of enclosing land for pasture and of taking over the arable and common land on which poor country people had for long relied for their subsistence. Kett's Rebellion was soon suppressed and Kett and his brother hanged; but the hesitant way in which Somerset had dealt with the growing crisis enabled his rival, the Earl of Warwick, later Duke of Northumberland, to take over the government in the name of the King whose health was failing fast.

Well aware that his fall from power was likely to be as

sudden as Somerset's if the King were to be succeeded by his half-sister and rightful heir, Mary – the devoutly Roman Catholic daughter of Catherine of Aragon – Northumberland endeavoured to secure a Protestant succession with the ready complicity of the dying King. He hastily arranged for the marriage of his son to Lady Jane Grey, the King's cousin and a granddaughter of a younger sister of Henry VIII.

On the afternoon of 6 July 1553, King Edward died at the age of fifteen, poisoned by the medicines that his physicians had prescribed, with swollen legs and arms and darkened skin, his fingers and toes touched by gangrene, his hair and nails falling out. Although she fainted when told that he had nominated her his successor, and then tearfully declared that she had no right to the Crown since the Lady Mary was 'the rightful heir', Lady Jane Grey eventually gave way to the entreaties of her relations and to what she was persuaded to believe was the will of God.

The English people were, however, not so ready to submit. Nor was Mary. From her castle at Framlingham, she sent an order to the Council demanding the recognition of her rights; and in this she was supported even by the Protestant citizens of London, exasperated as they were by the corruption and mismanagement of the Duke of Northumberland who had pillaged the Church as ruthlessly as Somerset, lavishing fortunes upon Dudley Castle in Staffordshire and his London house in Ely Place. Mary marched into London unopposed. Northumberland was arrested and executed; and so was Lady Jane Grey after her father's implication in a rebellion against Mary led by the reckless conspirator, Sir Thomas Wyatt.

Mary was a virtuous and conscientious woman who would have been quite well suited to the quiet, orderly, innocent life of a nun. Unworldly and impressionable, she was unshakeably loyal to those few people she loved and to the religion which was the mainstay of her life. Her reign was to be remembered for the screams of the Protestants on the crackling fires of Smithfield, the deaths of Hugh

Frontispiece to the *Book of Martyrs* by John Foxe, 1563.

The burning of Thomas Cranmer at Oxford in 1556, an illustration from Foxe's *Book of Martyrs*.

Latimer, former Bishop of Worcester, and Nicholas Ridley, Bishop of London, burned alive at Oxford, of Cranmer also burned at Oxford, and of those three hundred others whose martyrdom was to be commemorated by John Foxe in a book which – with its strong implication that the English people had been chosen by God to fight against anti-Christ in the person of the Pope – was later to be considered so important a work that it was ordained that copies should be available in all cathedrals, as well as in the houses of gentry and the upper clergy, for the edification of both servants and visitors.

Yet Mary who presided over this bloodshed was not cruel by nature. Obstinate and narrow-minded, she knew her way to God and could not conceive that there might be some other way. Men and women had to suffer for their refusal to accept it, not to be punished but to be saved. In vain did her husband advise her to be less rigorous, for political rather than religious considerations.

This husband was Philip II, King of Spain, a solemn, courteous young man whom she adored, the representative of all that she held most dear, her mother's country and her mother's faith. She longed to have a child by him so as to

Queen Mary, the Roman Catholic who reigned from 1553 to 1558.

Elizabeth I as a woman of about 42 years of age.

unite their two countries in blessed trinity with Rome. But all her hopes were in vain. Pregnancy after pregnancy proved illusory; her husband, eleven years younger than herself, returned to Spain, persuaded that his wife lacked 'all sensibility of the flesh'. She died in 1558 of cancer of the ovaries, miserable and unlamented, often in great pain, so fearful of assassination that she had taken to wearing armour, dragged by Spain into a war with France which resulted in the loss of Calais, England's last toehold on the Continent.

These were miserable times for England. The country was in economic decline, already plagued by those bands of unemployed, unruly vagabonds which were to present such an intractable problem throughout the coming years. Prices were rising; wages for most workers remained low, field-workers earning about twopence a day, the price they would have been asked to pay for a single rabbit. Men such as these looked with a kind of desperate hope to their new Queen, Anne Boleyn's daughter, Elizabeth, a pale, composed, simply-dressed Protestant girl who was said to have knelt down on the grass beneath an oak tree when told of her half-sister's death and her own accession and to have quoted in Latin the words from the 118th Psalm, 'This is the Lord's doing. It is marvellous in our eyes.'

Queen Elizabeth, twenty-five years old, was already a formidable personality. In a report to his master, the Spanish Ambassador in London described her as being 'incomparably more feared' by her advisers than her sister had been. She was also 'undoubtedly a very clever young woman' but 'extremely vain'. This was certainly true. She could read Latin and Greek with equal facility; she spoke French, Spanish and Italian as well as Latin and even a little Welsh. Roger Ascham, her tutor, had never known a pupil with a quicker apprehension or a more retentive memory. She could talk intelligently on any intellectual topic, and would spend three hours a day reading history. Yet, astute and alert as she was, she was susceptible to the most out-landish flattery. Even in old age when the smooth, reddish gold of her hair had given way to a wig and the remaining teeth in her wrinkled jaw were black and decayed, she expected the handsome men she liked to have about her court to tell her how beautiful she was, that they would die of passion for her, that they could not look upon her face for long for fear of being dazzled by its loveliness. Towards the end of her life the French Ambassador was disconcerted by her pulling open the front of her dress so that he could see her breasts and her belly 'even to the navel'.

Elizabeth opening her last Parliament.

She was exasperating as well as flirtatious, difficult and demanding, reluctant to make up her mind and constantly changing it, as eager to take all the credit for her govern-ment's successes as she was quick to shuffle the blame onto her ministers when things went wrong. Dictatorial and high-handed, selfish and ungrateful, she would irritably slap her ladies and even her ministers and councillors when they annoyed her. They all acknowledged her authority but often pursued policies in direct opposition to her wishes, keeping important documents from her sight and encourag-ing ambassadors to give her misleading reports. Fortunately they were for the most part themselves men of exceptional talent. Among them were Sir William Cecil, later Lord Burghley, industrious, trustworthy, a master of statecraft; Sir Francis Walsingham, the wily, brilliant organizer of a network of agents unparalleled in Europe; Sir Christopher Hatton, Lord Chancellor and skilled manipulator of the House of Commons. Her court was indeed a busy hive of genius where intellectual gifts and gallantry were valued more than high birth, where even those who were its most decorative and dashing denizens, like the handsome and adored Earl of Leicester, and Sir Walter Ralegh, soldier, navigator, poet, historian and chemist, were men of excep-tional ability. Musicians, artists and men of letters were encouraged at court as well as such adventurers as Hawkins, Frobisher and Sir Francis Drake who brought

William Cecil, 1st Baron Burghley, Elizabeth I's faithful minister.

English shipwrights
working on plans in
Elizabeth's time.

home great wealth from their voyages, delighting the
Queen, a most exact not to say parsimonious accountant,
by the enrichment of her coffers.

After the miseries of the previous reign it seemed, indeed,
a golden age, the age of Christopher Marlowe and Shakespeare, of Philip Sidney and Edmund Spenser, of Nicholas
Hilliard, Thomas Tallis, William Byrd and Orlando
Gibbons, and of Hakluyt's *Voyages and Discoveries of the
English Nation* which described the adventurous explo-
rations of the country's navigators, one of whose voyages –
James Lancaster's to the East Indies – led to the establishment of the East India Company and the beginnings of the
empire in India. Other voyages and discoveries were eventually to result in an even larger empire across the Atlantic
in America. Yet the Queen was the patron rather than the
begetter of the age. Her achievements have been exaggerated; her posthumous reputation is a triumph of propaganda over reason. The religious settlement, a compromise
of views – while welcome to those who shared the Queen's
own impatience with petty doctrinal squabbles – was as
unacceptable to the extreme Protestants known as Puritans,
as it was to ardent Catholics. Several times the Queen's life

was in danger from conspirators, most notable amongst whom was the beguiling Mary Queen of Scots, daughter of James V of Scotland and, through a descent untainted by illegitimacy, great-granddaughter of Henry VII. Once the King of France's wife, Mary Stuart was as troublesome to Elizabeth when living in Scotland as she was to be after she had been driven from that country by her Protestant lords who were outraged by her marriage to the Earl of Bothwell, murderer of her second husband, Lord Darnley. Queen Elizabeth did not shrink from having other conspirators tortured and then hanged, drawn and quartered as traitors. But Mary, as a queen and her cousin, she was reluctant to bring to trial; and it was not until her proven complicity in the plot of the Catholic would-be assassin, Anthony Babington, that Elizabeth consented to sign the Queen of Scots's death warrant, afterwards characteristically blaming others for its precipitate execution at Fotheringhay Castle in 1587.

A miniature by Nicholas Hilliard of Mary Queen of Scots.

The following year the Queen's throne seemed under even greater threat from the Spanish Armada, an immense fleet of ships and tens of thousands of soldiers sent with the blessing of the Pope to overthrow the heretical Queen of England, to bring her country back into the Catholic fold and to prevent British troops interfering in the Netherlands

The Spanish Armada of 1588 as embroidered on an early 18th-century tapestry.

A gold medal struck to commemorate England's victory over the Spanish fleet.

Elizabethan London showing shipping on the Thames, St. Paul's Cathedral, and the Globe theatre and Bear Garden in the foreground.

where Protestant rebels were in revolt against their Spanish masters. But the Spanish galleys proved no match for the more manoeuvrable smaller British ships and, having suffered heavy losses, they were dispersed by storms. Driven further and further north, the survivors of the catastrophe were forced to sail round Scotland and down the coast of Ireland where many of those who clambered ashore in the hope of salvation were robbed, murdered or held to ransom.

The danger over, the Queen – who had made a speech celebrated for its stirring patriotism to the troops assembled at Tilbury – returned to her familiar cheese-paring, denying money to her crews and adequate support to her naval commanders. Yet all over the realm, immense sums were being spent on houses built by men who had been allowed to make vast fortunes through the remunerative offices, monopolies and licences granted them by the Queen or who had made fortunes by their own often shady speculations in trade and finance. William Cecil, Lord Burghley, granted the immensely profitable office of Master of the Court of Wards, owned Burghley House in Lincolnshire as well as Theobalds, a house nearer London which he was obliged to enlarge considerably 'by occasion of Her Majesty's often coming'. Christopher Hatton, the Queen's Lord Chancellor, all but ruined himself building Holdenby House in Northamptonshire which stood ready for ten years, full of servants vainly waiting for the Queen to come to stay. The Earl of Leicester, the Master of the Horse, spent as large a fortune upon Kenilworth Castle, Warwickshire. Several of those who had made fortunes in her time, either through profitable offices or by such commercial enterprise as the export of woollen cloth, turned to Robert Smythson, mason and architect, to advise them in their designs, as did Sir Francis Willoughby of Wollaton Hall, Nottingham, Sir Henry Griffith of Burton Agnes, Humberside and the Countess of Shrewsbury in that dramatic combination of the Gothic and the classical, Hardwick Hall, Derbyshire.

Little Moreton Hall, Cheshire, a characteristic half-timbered manor house of the Tudor period.

Some of these houses were enormous, like Montacute near Yeovil, others, such as Sulgrave Manor, Oxfordshire, built in 1558 and occupied by members of the Washington family, were relatively small. Most were built of brick and stone; a few, like Little Moreton Hall, that astonishing black and white creation in Cheshire to which William Moreton added the jettied gatehouse in the 1550s, were of wood; many were in the shape of an E – supposedly in flattery of Elizabeth – as was Charlecote Park where William Shakespeare is said to have been caught on a poaching expedition, tried in the great hall and flogged on order of the house's owner, Sir Thomas Lucy, subsequently to be ridiculed as Justice Shallow.

The bedroom used by Elizabeth I at Burghley House, Lincolnshire.

Guido
Fawkes

Robert
Catesby

Previous page:
Contemporary engraving
of Guy Fawkes and the
Gunpowder Plot
Conspirators, 1605.

In her great bedchamber at Richmond Palace in the early morning of 24 March 1603 Queen Elizabeth turned her white and wrinkled face to the wall and died. Three hours later, as soon as it was light, a messenger galloped away to Edinburgh to inform her kinsman King James VI of Scotland, son of Mary Stuart, Queen of Scots, that he was King now, too, of England.

A few years later, after the arrival in London of this the first of the Stuart monarchs, Ben Jonson's *Masque of Augures* was performed in the recently completed Banqueting House in Whitehall. Nothing could have more fittingly symbolized the opening of a new age. The Banqueting House, designed by Inigo Jones and with a ceiling painted by Peter Paul Rubens, was the first purely Renaissance building to appear in London. While it was being built William Harvey, physician to St Bartholomew's Hospital, was working on the treatise which was to explain the circulation of the blood; William Gilbert's *De Magnete* had established the magnetic nature of the earth and founded the study of electrical science; John Donne, Dean of St Paul's, was writing the verse which proclaimed him the most notable poet of the metaphysical school; the Authorized Version of the Bible, recently completed, was already becoming recognized as a masterpiece of English prose; Francis Bacon was revising the great works which propounded his radical system of philosophy; the group of English Puritans known as the Pilgrim Fathers had just sailed in the *Mayflower* to North America and had established a flourishing colony in New England at New Plymouth, Massachusetts.

The king who now ruled in the country which they had left was not a man to command respect. Described by the duc de Sully as 'the wisest fool in Christendom', he was certainly most learned and as pedantic as he was undignified. Conceited and slovenly, he spoke in the 'full dialect of his country' and in a very loud voice, expressing his opinions with an 'exasperating dogmatism'. Terrified of witches and

James I, the first of the Stuart monarchs, who succeeded Elizabeth I in 1603.

124

naked steel, he hated the sea and pigs and wrote a diatribe against smoking, a habit now far more widespread than it had been in the recent past when a servant, seeing smoke emanating from Sir Walter Ralegh's mouth, had thrown a pot of ale over him, supposing him to be on fire.

Instead of occupying himself with the evils of smoking and witchcraft, and with the handsome young men about his court, it was felt that the King should expend more thought upon the needs of the navy – much neglected since the end of the long war with Spain – upon the problems of Ulster – where Presbyterians were being settled on lands from which the Catholic Irish were being expelled – and upon the growing discontent in England of Puritans and Catholics alike. In 1605 there had been a plot, engineered by Catholics, to blow King James and his ministers up in the Houses of Parliament where Guy Fawkes had planted barrels of gunpowder in the cellars, a ritual search of which is still made by the Yeomen of the Guard before the State Opening of Parliament.

Pipe smoking became a common habit in the early 17th century.

It was, however, not so much the Catholics as the radical Protestants whom the King saw as the 'chiefest enemies' of his authority and most of whose requests for reforms in the Anglican Church he firmly turned down at the Hampton Court Conference of 1604, rejecting their demands for changes in the government of the Church by bishops and in the Prayer Book, though agreeing to a new translation of the Bible which eventually appeared as the King James or Authorized Version in 1611.

His authority as King, James I insisted, was exercised by the ancient doctrine of divine right. He held that all his subjects should obey him as God's lieutenant on earth. Even women were required to kneel when presented to him; and Parliaments were regarded as mere instruments of the royal will, summoned to give their assent to royal decisions and to grant the money the government needed for the administration of the realm. Naturally most Members of Parliament were resentful of the low esteem in which the King evidently held them and the menial role in government to which he seemed determined to relegate them. More and more insistently, they were claiming the right to be consulted on important affairs of state, not to direct policy but at least to have a say in its formulation.

At odds with his first Parliament over money matters, the King dissolved it and contrived to manage without another for ten years, raising money by selling peerages and baronetcies. He was driven to summon Parliament again in 1621 by shortage of money, but the unresolved disputes over the Members' right to be consulted as to the purposes to which the finances the King demanded were to be put, soon resulted in further quarrels; and once more the King sent them home, complaining of their insolence, resolute in his determination that Parliament should not presume to take more power into its hands than he deemed appropriate, that its functions should mainly be limited, as they had been in the Middle Ages, to voting the monarch the finances necessary for the conduct of the affairs of the realm. King James died soon after this last quarrel with his Parliament, leaving his son, Charles I, to cope with a problem which was to be resolved only by his own violent death.

Charles I had many admirable qualities but he inspired more respect than affection. His grave reserve, fastidious constraint and lack of humour were barriers to intimacy that all but a very few found it impossible to cross. His slight stammer, which in another man might have been appealing, was in him merely a defect which made it the more difficult for him to put strangers at their ease, seeming to emphasize the atmosphere of melancholy that surrounded him, a melancholy so well conveyed in Van Dyck's *Charles I in Three Positions* that when Bernini saw the portrait he described the countenance depicted as a countenance 'doomed'. 'Never,' the sculptor said, 'never have I beheld features more unfortunate.'

Charles was a studious rather than an intelligent man. He understood books better than people, and seemed incapable

Triple portrait of Charles I
by Van Dyck.

of making that kind of contact with his subjects which had ensured such popularity for the young Elizabeth I. With Parliament his dealings were from the start disastrous. Believing no less firmly than his father in the divine right of kings, he treated Parliament with a shy and distant reserve which seemed like contempt. Its Members, increasingly Puritan in sympathy, regarded both him and his foreign Catholic wife, his intimate friend, the Duke of Buckingham, as well as his High Church allegiance and his foreign entanglements, with the utmost suspicion. When asked to vote him the usual import duties for life, they declined to do so, granting them for one year only. The King responded by dissolving Parliament, collecting the customs duties which had been denied him, raising a forced loan and threatening those who refused to pay with imprisonment. Compelled once more by shortage of money to call another Parliament in 1628, he found himself faced by a formidable opposition led by Sir John Eliot whom he had arrested and thrown into the Tower, but not before he had been forced to accept a Petition of Right which forbade the levying of taxes without parliamentary consent, and not before his dear friend, the Duke of Buckingham, had been murdered.

127

After Parliament's dissolution, Charles managed by various financial expediences to survive for eleven years without calling another until 1640 when, having tried to impose his High Church practices north of the Tweed, a rebellious Scottish army marched into England. Another Parliament was now essential; and so the Members of what was to become known as the Long Parliament assembled at Westminster.

Immediately they ordered the arrests of the Earl of Strafford, the King's most ruthlessly efficient minister, and of William Laud, his Archbishop of Canterbury, 'a little low red-faced man of mean parentage', in the words of one of his many enemies, unimaginative and outspoken, sometimes irritable and often rude, a passionate upholder of High Church doctrines. After the King had been obliged to consent to the execution of Strafford – who was later followed to the scaffold by Laud – the drift into violent conflict between Crown and Parliament was much accelerated. A whole series of measures were introduced by the Long Parliament limiting the authority of the Crown while increasing its own. These measures were passed without undue difficulty; but plans for religious changes revealed wide differences of opinion among Members. So did a Militia Bill which proposed the transfer of military command from the Crown to Parliament, and a Grand Remonstrance – brought forward by John Pym and other leaders of the House of Commons – which urged radical reforms in the Church, including the curbing of the power of bishops, and the replacement of the King's counsellors by ministers approved by Parliament. This was too much for the King to tolerate. Having hesitated too long, he now went too far. Leading a party of swordsmen, he marched to the Commons to arrest Pym and four other Members. When he arrived there, he discovered that 'all the birds [were] flown'. They had escaped to the City where the authorities refused to deliver them up. War was now inevitable; and on 22 August 1642 in a field near

Nottingham King Charles unfurled his standard beneath a glowering sky.

At that time there were scarcely more than a thousand men at his command; and many of those who had declared their allegiance shared the reluctance of Sir Edmund Verney – shortly to be killed fighting for the King in Warwickshire – who declared, 'I do not like the quarrel and heartily wish the King would yield.' Many who might have supported the King, if only out of the simple loyalty displayed by Verney, hung back: it was harvest time for one thing; and, for another, the King was still making overtures to Parliament as though he hoped, even now, to reach a compromise. Men were reluctant to jeopardize their future by openly declaring their support of a cause which might at any moment be abandoned or betrayed by a man so widely distrusted because of his underhand dealings and prevaricating manner. But then Parliament declared that all men who did not support it were 'delinquents' and that their property was forfeit. This meant that those who would have been happy to stay neutral were virtually obliged to fight in their own defence; and men whose fortunes might have been lost had Parliament won, now undertook to raise troops to fight for the King in whose victory their own salvation might be secured.

If self-interest provided the spur for this early surge of support for the Royalist cause, other reasons, no less vital, played their part in swelling the numbers of men who eventually decided to throw in their lot with the King. It was not only that the King's majesty was considered by many to be sacrosanct. There was also the strong feeling that King Charles was the defender of the true Church, as he himself contended, anxious as he was to steer a steady and true course between the rocks of popery on the one hand and Puritanism on the other. He had read with admiration Richard Montague's *Appelo Caesarem* which identified popery with tyranny, and Puritanism with anarchy, and which concluded 'popery is originall of Superstition; puritanisme, the high-way unto prophaneness; both alike [are] enemies unto piety.' This stated the King's own views precisely. He had abhorred the priests of his Roman Catholic wife; he regarded with even more distaste the opinions of the Puritan landowners and merchants in the House of Commons and the Puritan preachers whose disrupting and often rabidly Protestant sermons could be heard all over London. It was his belief, no less than it had been his father's, that an attack on the bishops was an attack on the King. Moreover, while the Civil War was never primarily a class struggle – the gentry were fairly equally divided – there was an undeniable fear among many of the King's supporters that the lower classes would use this opportunity to turn upon their masters, that the predominantly Puritan merchants and shopkeepers of the towns were intent upon upsetting the structure of power to their own advantage, that the King's opponents represented rebellion and chaos as opposed to law and order. These feelings were strongest in the north, except for the industrialized parts of Yorkshire and Lancashire, in the West Midlands and Wales, and in the West Country. Parliament, on the other hand, derived its strongest support from south-east England and London.

The great hall of Littlecote House, Berkshire, its walls decorated with weapons and uniforms of Parliamentary troops who were billeted here in the Civil War.

But there were no clear lines of division. Hundreds of families were split in their loyalties; many changed from side to side with the fortunes of war; while thousands of country people found themselves drawn into the conflict on the side that their landlords and masters elected to support. Thousands more were not too sure what all the fuss was about or did not really care what government they lived under so long as they could plough their fields and go to market. Only three men in every hundred took an active part in the conflict; and some did not even know there was a conflict at all. Long after the first battles had been fought, a Yorkshire farm labourer, when advised to keep out of the line of fire between the King's men and Parliament's, learned for the first time that 'them two had fallen out'.

Charles I's nephew, Prince Rupert, the Royalists' leading cavalry commander.

Largely because of their preponderance in cavalry, it seemed at first that the King's men, or Cavaliers, as they consequently became known, would triumph; and had the commander of their horse, the King's young nephew, Prince Rupert of the Rhine, been less impetuous, they might well have won an important victory in the first indecisive battle at Edgehill. Thereafter the fortunes of the Royalists began to decline and the tide turned in favour of the Parliamentarians or Roundheads as they were known because of their close cropped hair which was in marked contrast to the flowing locks of the Cavaliers. The stout and stolid Earl of Essex whom the Parliamentarians had placed in command of their army, was eclipsed by men of far more outstanding talent, by John Hampden, the influential Member of Parliament for Buckinghamshire, who was mortally wounded at Chalgrove Field, by the cavalry leader, Lord Fairfax, by Henry Ireton, the young Nottinghamshire lawyer who was one of the King's most implacable enemies, and, above all, by Ireton's father-in-law, Oliver Cromwell, a clumsy farmer from Huntingdon with heavy-lidded eyes, a face marred by warts and a large nose, Member of Parliament for Cambridge, and recognized by both sides in the conflict as a man of unswerving fixity of purpose

Oliver Cromwell, the Parliamentary general who became Lord Protector in 1653.

and powerful, self-confident patriotism. 'His linen was plain and not very clean,' wrote a Member of Parliament who heard him speaking in the House of Commons for the first time; 'and I remember a speck or two of blood upon his little band which was not much larger than his collar. His hat was without a hat band. His stature was of a good size, his sword stuck close to his side; his countenance swollen and reddish; his voice sharp and untunable, and his eloquence full of fervour.'

'Pray, Mr Hampden,' another Member had once been asked by a colleague intrigued by Cromwell's rough-skinned face with its conspicuous mole beneath his lower lip and his generally dishevelled appearance, 'Pray, who is that sloven?' 'That sloven,' Hampden had replied, 'that sloven whom you see before you hath no ornament in his speech; but that sloven, I say, if we should ever come to a breach with the King, in such a case, I say, that sloven will be the greatest man in England.'

So it proved to be. By his defeat at Marston Moor, the King lost the north; at Naseby he lost most of his army; and after the battle of Preston, it became ever more clear that he would lose his head. This he did on a scaffold outside the windows of the Banqueting House on a bitterly cold

Troops drawn up for battle on 14 June 1645 at Naseby, Northamptonshire, where the Royalists were decisively defeated.

The execution of Charles I outside the Banqueting House, Whitehall, on 30 January 1649.

January day in 1649; and Oliver Cromwell, who had signed the death warrant of the royal 'Tyrant, Traitor, Murderer and Public Enemy', became, indeed, the greatest man in England.

Dealing ruthlessly with his other enemies, he imprisoned or shot mutineers in his army; crushed without mercy a rebellion in Ireland; routed the Scots who had proclaimed Charles I's son their King; won a final victory over his enemies in September 1651 at Worcester; constructed a fleet with which Admiral Blake defeated the Dutch; suppressed the Levellers who, led by John Lilburne, proposed a radical political programme not at all to his taste; and furiously dissolved the so-called Rump, the ineffective remnant of the Long Parliament that had survived a purge by one of his officers, Colonel Thomas Pride, a London brewer's drayman, who had arrested or excluded over a hundred dissident Members.

Cromwell replaced the Rump with an assembly largely chosen by himself; but this lasted a few months only, and in December 1653, by an Instrument of Government, he became Lord Protector of the Commonwealth of England. Ruling increasingly by decree, he instituted direct military rule by dividing the country into eleven districts commanded by major-generals.

Severe as Cromwell's rule was, it was a generally benevo-

Reverse of the Great Seal of England showing the House of Commons in session during the Commonwealth.

133

lent despotism which allowed a large measure of intellectual freedom and religious toleration, permitting the Jews to return to England. But it was also a joyless one which witnessed the wanton destruction of numerous treasures in churches and cathedrals throughout the country on the grounds that they were 'graven images', condemned to destruction, like the heads of the lovely medieval statues and the painted windows in the Lady Chapel at Ely Cathedral.

When the Lord Protector died, and was succeeded by his son, Richard, the regime began immediately to collapse. One of his generals, George Monck, later Duke of Albemarle, occupied London, and arranged for new parliamentary elections. The Parliament thus elected in 1660 resolved the crisis by asking the late King's son to return from his long exile in France as King Charles II.

The experiment with republicanism was over. Parliament proclaimed that 'according to the ancient and fundamental laws of this kingdom, the government is, and ought to be, by king, lords and commoners'. Yet, although a king was once more to sit upon the throne, the struggle for power had ended only superficially in the monarchy's favour. There was to be no return to the absolute rule of the king. Just as

Cromwell forcibly dissolving the so-called 'Rump' of the Long Parliament in April 1653.

Cromwell supervising the destruction of the monarchy, symbolized by 'the Royall Oake'.

the father had been defeated, so too might the son be. Parliament had established not only its right to financial control but also its right to be consulted on foreign policy and religion as well as trade and domestic affairs. In the future the problem for the monarch was not how to defeat Parliament but how to influence the rival political parties that alternately controlled a majority of its seats, until the monarch was seen to be above the strife altogether.

THE RISE AND FALL OF EMPIRE

From the Restoration of the Monarchy (1660)
to the England of today

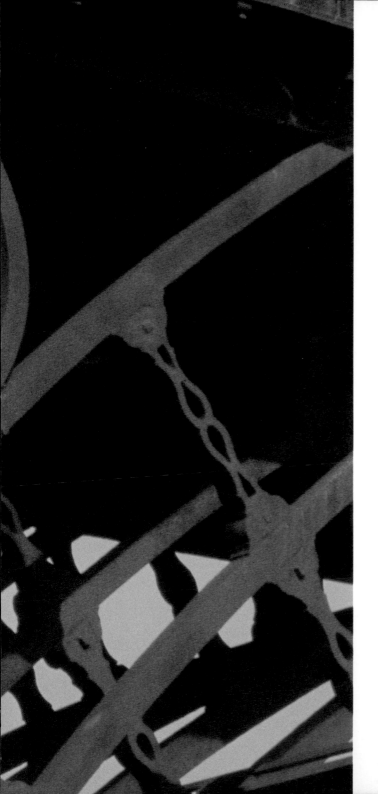

'The shouting and joy expressed by all' at King Charles II's restoration to the throne was, so Samuel Pepys recorded in his diary, 'past imagination'. There were fireworks and bonfires and dancing in the streets; church bells rang and cannon roared as the King rode into the capital accompanied by an immense retinue of gentlemen in doublets of cloth of silver and velvet coats, of footmen in purple liveries, and soldiers in buff uniforms trimmed with silver lace. Not only royalists but all except the most diehard republicans welcomed the return of the monarchy, and they were not to be disappointed. The new King showed himself anxious to placate his former enemies as well as to reward his friends. They were given offices at court and in government impartially; and the protection of an Act of Indemnity and Oblivion was extended to everyone except those who had signed Charles I's death warrant and a very few others.

The curtains of reopened theatres rose upon comedies by William Wycherley, Congreve and Dryden. The King himself founded two theatre companies in Covent Garden where Inigo Jones's piazza and his church of St Paul's had been built some thirty years before; and he became, either personally or through his friends, one of London's greatest benefactors. He laid the foundation stone of the Royal Hospital, Chelsea which was designed by Christopher Wren whose first work, the Sheldonian Theatre, had recently been completed at Oxford. He had the Queen's

The coronation procession of Charles II, who was restored to the throne in 1660.

Chapel, opposite St James's Palace refurnished for his Portuguese wife, Catherine of Braganza. He extended the royal aviary, the site of the present Birdcage Walk, and he improved Constitution Hill which is believed to have got its name from his habit of taking walks there. He began a new palace at Greenwich which, designed by Inigo Jones's pupil, John Webb, is now the Royal Naval College; and at Windsor he employed the architect, Hugh May, to rebuild the State Apartments where the delicately painted ceilings by the Neapolitan Antonio Verrio and the richly carved cornices and frames by Grinling Gibbons were much admired by the King, whose taste for the exuberant and sensuous style known as Baroque had been formed in Paris and Versailles. He granted land in the area known as Soho after the ancient hunting cry, to his friend Henry Jermyn, Earl of St Albans, who was also given several acres in St James's where a highly fashionable area was developed including The Mall, Pall Mall, and several other streets around St James's Square, all named after members of the King's family or servants.

West of this development, Hyde Park and Green Park were made into royal parks; while André Le Notre, whose work the King had admired in France, was commissioned to lay out afresh St James's Park where Charles's tall, graceful figure could often be seen strolling about with his dogs and mistresses. Le Notre was also employed in laying out Greenwich Park where Wren was asked to design the Royal Observatory for the Astronomer Royal, Sir John Flamsteed.

It was the King's interest in scientific matters which induced the diarist and virtuoso, John Evelyn, to suggest that the groups of scientists and philosophers who met regularly at Gresham College to discuss the 'Advancement of Natural Science' should be formally instituted as the Royal Society. Among the Society's members, apart from Wren, Evelyn and Flamsteed, were John Aubrey, the antiquary, Robert Boyle, the physicist and chemist, Sir William Petty, the founder of population statistics, John Locke, the

Nell Gwynn, former orange girl at the Theatre Royal, who became Charles II's most celebrated mistress.

141

Grave diggers at work during one of London's outbreaks of plague.

philosopher, and Isaac Newton, the greatest scientist of his age. Nothing, indeed, could have better illustrated the transformation of English society – the emphasis upon science and secular political philosophy at the expense of theological disquisition and religious enthusiasm – than the King's granting official recognition to the Society by its royal charter and his approval of its purposes by his attendance at the Society's meetings. Such patronage did not go uncensured; and when the Great Plague of 1664-5, the fearful climax of a series of epidemics, claimed thousands of victims in London, and when, soon afterwards, much of the City of London was destroyed by a raging fire, there were those who claimed that these dreadful visitations were God's angry punishments of a people steeped in sin and preoccupied with 'blasphemous questionings'.

The Great Fire presented the authorities with an opportunity for building the kind of Italianate city with wide streets and spacious piazzas proposed by John Evelyn. The opportunity was lost; but there did emerge among the ruins of the old city several beautiful churches, livery halls and other buildings by Christopher Wren and his assistant, Nicholas Hawksmoor, as well as Wren's masterpiece, St Paul's Cathedral.

Sir Christopher Wren, mathematician, astronomer and the most accomplished architect of his time.

Worship in most of these churches was now conducted in accordance with the Anglican rites which Archbishop Laud had favoured and was accompanied by the music to be heard in the Chapel Royal at St James's Palace where the young Henry Purcell – soon to be hailed as the finest composer his country had ever produced – was then a chorister.

The King himself was not a devout man. He could be seen in his chapel asleep during the sermons or gazing fondly at some wanton mistress, or, on one occasion at least, kneeling to receive Holy Communion with three bishops on one side of him and three illegitimate sons by three different women on the other. Yet, while making fun of Nonconformists, and having scant sympathy with John Milton – champion of the Puritan revolution whose later works, written at this

142

time, are imbued with despair – or with John Bunyan – author of *The Pilgrim's Progress*, begun in prison where he languished for refusing to accept the new regulations against Dissenters – the King strongly advocated leniency towards Catholics and, pending parliamentary approval, promised to use his royal prerogative to relieve them of the restrictions under which they laboured. In 1672, when Parliament withheld its consent, he arbitrarily suspended the penal laws altogether. Parliament intervened, passing the Test Act which, besides requiring office holders to receive the Anglican communion, obliged them to repudiate the Catholic doctrine of transubstantiation.

Religious differences came to a head when Charles II died and, leaving no legitimate heir, was succeeded by his brother, James II, an avowed Catholic. An enthusiastic and tirelessly energetic adulterer, James had few other vices, apart from an impenetrable obstinacy, but his virtues were not attractive ones. Sincere but self-righteous, a firm friend but a 'heavy enemy', industrious but unimaginative and humourless, his principal objects in life were the conversion of England to Roman Catholicism and the establishment of a monarchy on the model of Louis XIV's. And after the defeat of rebel forces led by one of Charles II's illegitimate sons, the Duke of Monmouth, and the savage punishment of the survivors by the Lord Chief Justice, George Jeffreys, the King set his mind to the realization of his objectives. He admitted Catholics into his large army and into the universities; and in 1687 he issued his Declaration of Indulgence suspending the penal laws against them. Seven bishops who defied an order to read this declaration in all Anglican churches the following year were prosecuted and acquitted to tumultuous rejoicing; and after the birth of a prince threatened a Catholic dynasty, an invitation was sent by seven leading statesmen to William of Orange, James's Dutch nephew, a grave, shrewd Protestant and the husband of Mary, James's daughter by his first wife.

William landed at Torbay on 15 November 1688 and

The Roman Catholic James II succeeded his brother, Charles II, in 1685.

A playing card representing the execution of three of the conspirators involved in the Popish Plot of 1678, a fictitious Jesuit plot to assassinate Charles II.

The Execution of the mur: therers of Sᵗ EB Godfree

The Protestant William III came to the throne after the deposition of James II in the Glorious Revolution of 1688.

marched upon London as James's few supporters deserted him and he himself fled to France. The Glorious Revolution was thus achieved without bloodshed; and William and Mary jointly accepted the Bill of Rights which, excluding any Roman Catholic from the succession, confirmed the principle of parliamentary supremacy and guaranteed free speech within both the House of Lords and the House of Commons. On their acceptance of this Bill, William and Mary were crowned jointly in Westminster Abbey; and, in the defeat of what was taken to be Roman Catholic despotism, the age of constitutional monarchy, of a monarchy with powers limited by Parliament, began. The revolution which brought about this shift in power has been, and continues to be variously interpreted. For the nineteenth-century historian, Lord Macaulay, it was the most important event in modern history, ensuring that England was spared the revolutions that were to break out in other European countries. Later historians have tended to question its credentials as a revolution at all, either because ordinary people were only incidentally involved in it or because it was bloodless, though it led to bloodshed in Scotland where William III's troops fought the Jacobites, as supporters of James II and his heirs were known, and in Ireland where William defeated them at the battle of the Boyne in July 1690. Yet certain it is that after 1688 Parliament had to be summoned every year and not just when the monarch needed its help. The Crown still had formidable rights, not least in the choice of government ministers; but the struggle for power had taken a decisive turn in Parliament's favour.

For years the English had been at loggerheads with the Dutch from whom they had seized New Amsterdam in 1664, renaming it New York. Rivals in trade as well as in colonial expansion, the Dutch had also been exemplars to English merchants, providing them with models for the English banking system and the financial operations conducted at the Royal Exchange which had recently been rebuilt to the designs of Edward Jarman after the destruction of the earlier building in the Great Fire.

Now the Dutch were to be the allies of the English in the War of the Spanish Succession, a European war vigorously promoted by King William III in his determination to foil Louis XIV's attempt to place his grandson upon the Spanish throne. The War lasted for thirteen years, and by the time it was over both William and Mary were dead; Mary's sister Anne had become Queen; and the Duke of Marlborough had been rewarded for his splendid victories on the Continent by the grant of the royal manor of Woodstock where John Vanbrugh, architect of Castle Howard and Seaton Delaval, built Blenheim Palace. To help pay for the cost of the war the window tax had been introduced, a tax resulting in the bricked-up windows still to be seen in the walls of many eighteenth- and early nineteenth-century houses. By the Treaties of Utrecht which ended the war in 1714, the year of Queen Anne's death, France ceded to England much of her territory in North America, while the English also obtained various islands in the West Indies and a monopoly of the South American slave trade, as well as Gibraltar and Minorca as part of their share of the dismantled Spanish Empire. England, or Great Britain as she had become by the Act of Union with the Scots in 1707, had

The grand Baroque Blenheim Palace, designed by Vanbrugh for the Duke and Duchess of Marlborough, was completed in 1722.

Early 18th-century view of
the docks and quay at
Bristol, for long England's
second greatest city.

emerged from the war as a world power. She had also
emerged as a trading nation with rapidly expanding resources and ever-growing export markets not only for textiles, for long the staple product of English workshops, but
also for raw materials and for newer manufactures, from
the output of foundries to weapons, tools and household
goods. Industrial output was soaring. The merchant marine
increased from 3300 vessels in 1702 to 9400 in 1776, and
trade with the colonies created the largest free trade area in
the world. Those working hard in England to supply this
market were poorly paid, but prices were also low and
remained so until the 1760s; the average worker in both
town and country was better off, if only slightly better, in
the middle of the century than he had been at the beginning.

At the same time the population of the country, still
mainly employed in agriculture, was growing fast. In 1600
there had been about four million people in England and
Wales. By the end of the century this number had risen to
about 5,500,000, by 1780 to some 7,500,000 and by 1800
to nearly nine million. London's population of 375,000 in

1650 rose to some 575,000 by 1700 and to almost a million by 1800, when it was not only the biggest town in England but the biggest in the world.

Towards the end of September 1735, Sir Robert Walpole moved into the house which had been granted to him as First Lord of the Treasury, Number Ten, Downing Street. A tall, stout, good-natured, rather coarse Norfolk squire, who never entirely lost his provincial accent though he had been to Eton and King's College, Cambridge, Walpole had by then become an indispensable minister of the Crown, indeed the first Prime Minister, a title which was not, however, officially recognized until later. He was a Whig, that is to say a member of the ruling oligarchy of men whose authority was based on their ascendancy in local government and whose influence had helped to secure the succession of the German Protestant King George I, Elector of Hanover, upon the death of Queen Anne, his distant relative, none of whose many children had survived. The Whigs' rivals, the Tories – whose name like theirs was originally an obscure term of abuse and whose supporters often described themselves as the Church party since they were warmly regarded by the Anglican squires of the shires – had become associated with the Jacobites, supporters of the claim of King James II's progeny, and so were anathema to George I, who clearly preferred Hanover to England, never troubled to learn much English, and was content to leave the government in the capable if not over-scrupulous hands of Sir Robert Walpole, an astute businessman and political manipulator whose acumen restored public confidence in the government after the bursting of the 'South Sea Bubble', the disastrous failure of a joint-stock company formed to trade, mainly in slaves, with Spanish America.

The people as a whole, as well as the King, satisfied that the law was reconciled with liberty, were content to see the country governed in the name of the House of Hanover, by Whig ministers supported in office by Whigs in Parliament, a Jacobite rising in 1715 being easily suppressed. There was another Jacobite rebellion in 1745; but, although this caused alarm for a time, when an army led by King James II's grandson, the Young Pretender, 'Bonnie Prince Charlie', marched down into England from Scotland, the rebels soon lost heart because of their lack of support, turned back at Derby, and in a battle at Culloden, near Inverness – the last land battle to be fought in Britain – were slaughtered by the King's son, the Duke of Cumberland.

There was discontent in these years, of course, and widespread poverty: it was the age of Hogarth's *Gin Lane*; of the warnings of Henry Fielding, the novelist and Bow Street magistrate, that if spirit drinking continued at its present rate there would soon be few poor people left to drink it; of the underworld of Gay's *Beggar's Opera*; of lunatics chained and mocked in Bedlam; of prisoners starved in Newgate; and of a savage penal code that condemned all kinds of malefactors to death by hanging.

But it was also the world of Handel and Canaletto, of Thomas Gainsborough and Joshua Reynolds, of Thomas Gray and Oliver Goldsmith, and of Richard ('Beau') Nash, master of ceremonies at Bath where the architect John Wood and his son were providing the city with such masterpieces of neo-classicism as the Circus and the Royal

'Gin Lane', William Hogarth's pictorial sermon on the evils of excessive spirit drinking in mid-18th-century London.

Crescent. It was, in fact, a world now inescapably associated with the term Georgian, a word not used in this sense until the beginning of the next century but signifying an elegant style of architecture and decoration strongly influenced by the buildings of the ancient Romans and Greeks. The Grand Tour – that continental journey which was an essential part of a gentleman's education in an age when the universities were at a low ebb – was introducing the rich to the glories of Renaissance architecture and to the works of such Italian masters as Andrea Palladio and Vincenzo Scamozzi, whose influence on English taste was to be so profound. Sir Robert Walpole himself built his Norfolk country house, Houghton Hall, in the grand Palladian style; and this was to be followed by numerous other great country houses whose owners and architects had been inspired by Italian models encountered on the Grand Tour, among them Colen Campbell's Stourhead, Lord Burlington's Chiswick House, west of London, Holkham Hall built for Thomas Coke, later Earl of Leicester, and Hagley Hall designed by Sanderson Miller for the first Lord Lyttelton. Other houses were built by men of more humble birth who had made fortunes in India, like Claremont, designed for Robert Clive by Lancelot 'Capability' Brown – whose landscaping transformed the parks of so many country houses – and Sezincote, built in the Indian manner by Samuel Pepys Cockerell for a brother who had been in the service of the East India Company.

The British Empire in India and elsewhere was much increased by the victories of the Seven Years' War against France. By his triumph at Plassey in 1757 against the pro-French Siraj-ud-Dawlah, ruler of Bengal, Robert Clive had established British ascendancy in Bengal; by his defeat of the French at Quebec two years later, James Wolfe had won Canada; and by the Treaty of Paris, which brought the war to a close in 1763, Britain was seen as the world's leading

The portico on the east front of Chiswick House, Lord Burlington's Palladian villa of 1725-9.

The Royal Crescent, Bath, a realization of Palladian grace, built to the designs of John Wood the Younger in 1767-74.

James Gillray's 1792 caricature of 'the Bottomless Pitt', a satire on the Prime Minister's exaggerated attenuation below the waist.

George III had to consign authority to his son as Prince Regent in 1811 when incapacitated by porphyria.

colonial power with footholds in Africa and islands in the West Indies as well as dominions in north America and Asia.

Robert Walpole, ill-suited to leading a government in time of war, had long since died; and the victories owed as much to the brilliant statesmanship of William Pitt, Earl of Chatham, the Prime Minister, as they did to the generals in the field. George I had also died and had been succeeded by his son, George II, who, towards the end of his life, was content to leave the government largely in the hands of his ministers. This was a policy not to the taste of his grandson, George III, an honest and kindly man with a most obstinate sense of duty, ill-advised by his mother and his 'dearest friend' and chief minister, the handsome and unexceptional Earl of Bute, to exercise to the full such royal powers as remained to him, particularly in the choice of ministers and in the exercise of patronage, the right to control the appointment to various offices, above all to offices presented to Members of Parliament, by which the Crown could manipulate voting in both Houses.

George III's attempts to rule through the 'King's friends' rather than through the Whig oligarchy and the Cabinet, the committee of the leading members of the government, which the Whigs controlled, soon led the well-meaning King into difficulties. One of his most scurrilous and effective opponents was the demagogue, John Wilkes, the 'most wicked and agreeable fellow' whom William Pitt had ever met. A profligate rake of great intelligence who charmed even Samuel Johnson, Wilkes was both a Member of Parliament and founder of the *North Briton*, a waspish periodical which the government attempted to suppress. Expelled from Parliament, he was three times re-elected by the defiant constituents of Middlesex; and by the time the American rebels had challenged the authority of King George III's government by their Declaration of Independence of 4 July 1776, Wilkes, together with Charles James Fox and Edmund Burke, had become one of the most outspoken opponents of government policies in the House of Commons.

Provoked by the government's persistent determination to tax their colonies and to oblige them to accept imported tea from the surplus stocks of the East India Company, the American rebels had first protested by tarring and feathering royal officials; then, disguised as Mohawks, by hurling chests of tea into Boston harbour. Eventually they demonstrated their determination to resist the royal troops by force of arms. Although a large proportion of Americans remained loyalist in sentiment, and although the King's troops won most of the battles fought in the War of Independence, the idea that the British army could subdue a continent at such a distance from its own shores was, as the Adjutant-General put it, as 'wild an idea as ever controverted common sense'. After the surrender at Yorktown in October 1781 of General Lord Cornwallis to George Washington and his French allies, victory for the United States was assured.

The year before London had been the terrifying scene of the worst riots in English history when an anti-Catholic demonstration, representing an age-old prejudice against papists as probably traitorous adherents of a foreign religion, was exploited by political activists, criminal gangs and workers with grudges against 'the wage-cutting blacklegs' of Roman Catholic Irishmen. At least 700 people lost their lives and the damage done to property was incalculable. 'Such a time of terror,' Samuel Johnson told Mrs Thrale, 'you have been fortunate in not seeing.' After the suppression of the riots – which George III threatened to put down in person at the head of his Guards since the magistrates appeared to be too frightened to do their duty – there were familiar calls for the establishment of a professional police force, and for various measures designed to repress a possible rebellion of an unruly working class. These calls were repeated a few years later when it was

Horatio Nelson, England's greatest and vainest admiral.

A caricature of the Commander-in-Chief, the Duke of Wellington, who gave his name to varieties of trees and apples as well as boots.

feared that repercussions from the Revolution in France would disturb the stability of England. It was at this time that Parliament passed the Combination Acts forbidding the forming of two or more people into a union for the purpose of obtaining a wage increase or better working conditions. But it was from the Revolution's heir, Napoleon Bonaparte, who threatened the country from without, rather than from such English working-class revolutionaries as the Luddites, who smashed the machines which were putting men out of work, that the real danger to the country came; and, while a series of towers – known as Martello Towers, after the tower at Cap Mortella where British troops had fought in Corsica – were built along the southern and western coasts, urgent efforts were made to bring the navy up to a strength capable of resisting the French invasion forces. After Lord Nelson's brilliant victories over the French fleet, culminating in his triumph at Trafalgar in 1805, there was no reason to fear a French invasion. Nor, after his final defeat at Waterloo in Belgium in 1815 at the hands of the Duke of Wellington and Marshal Blücher, was there any reason to fear Napoleon himself who died in captivity on the island of St Helena in 1821.

To tease the Duke of Wellington, it used to amuse George III's eldest son to extol his own prowess in leading heroic cavalry charges at Waterloo. 'In my life,' the Duke complained, 'I never heard so much nonsense and folly and so many lies in the same space of time.' This imaginative liar had been appointed Regent in 1811 when his father, suffering from the rare disease known as porphyria, displayed symptoms of insanity; and so the Regent gave his name to that exuberant style known as Regency, a neo-classical style based on Greek rather than Roman and on Egyptian and Chinese models. It was a style that might, indeed, have been specifically designed for the flamboyant and extravagant Regent himself who became King George IV on his father's death in 1820.

Exasperating as Wellington so often found the unpredictable 'blackguard', George IV, the Duke was forced to conclude that he was not only 'devilish entertaining' but 'a most magnificent patron of arts.' There was, indeed, scarcely a notable writer or artist of his time that George IV did not encourage and support. Even Byron, who joined in the general vilification of his selfishness, extravagance and lazy dissipation, had to admit that the King, that 'leviathan of the *haut ton*', had an impeccable taste in literature. He never lost an opportunity to praise the work of Sir Walter Scott and kept a set of Jane Austen's novels in 'every one of his residences'. As a lavish patron of English artists, he bought paintings by John Constable, sat for Nathaniel Dance, Cosway and Reynolds, commissioned works from Gainsborough, Stubbs, Hoppner, Romney and scores of other painters and sculptors, including Thomas Lawrence – whose fine portraits of Napoleon's enemies now hang in the Waterloo Chamber at Windsor Castle – and Canova whose splendid and colossal marble statue of Napoleon himself, presented by the King to Wellington, can now be seen at the Wellington Museum, Apsley House. Others of George IV's acquisitions now hang in the National Gallery, whose foundation in Trafalgar Square owes much to the King's enthusiastic support and whose imposing portico came from the Prince's sumptuous residence, Carlton House, in Pall Mall.

The rest of this grand house was demolished in the King's lifetime, Carlton House Terrace being built upon its site and in its gardens. At the same time the King's favourite architect, John Nash, was commissioned to build an even finer palace to take its place. This new palace, Buckingham Palace, was not finished until long after the King was dead. But George IV did live to see the realization of most of Nash's marvellous designs for Regent's Park and Regent Street in which he took the closest interest. He also saw to completion Nash's gorgeous Brighton Pavilion which took the place of an earlier Graeco-Roman style seaside house and was decorated and furnished for him in an Oriental

Gillray's caricature of the Prince Regent after a heavy meal at Carlton House in 1792.

The Prince Regent's extravagantly oriental Marine Pavilion at Brighton, built for him by John Nash in 1815-22.

A bricklayer's labourer at work in 1827.

style of exotic grandeur. Its cost, as the Princess de Lieven said, was 'really incredible'; yet, even so, was meagre when compared with the sum lavished upon the reconstruction of Windsor Castle where, year after year from 1823 to 1830, with cavalier disregard of the sums allocated by Parliament, armies of workmen under the direction of Jeffry Wyatville laboured to give the Castle its present appearance of solid yet romantic grandeur that has made it one of the most distinctive monuments in the world.

George IV concerned himself not only with the arts, In the sciences too, his patronage was eagerly sought and gratefully welcomed. He was President of the Royal Institution and bestowed knighthoods on both William Herschel, the astronomer, and Humphry Davy, the chemist and inventor of the safety lamp, one of those many English scientists who were helping to make Britain the workshop of the world and playing their essential part in that social and economic transformation known as the Industrial Revolution.

In 1775, when the Industrial Revolution was gathering momentum, Adam Smith, the political economist, was elected a member of The Club. On its foundation, at the instigation of Joshua Reynolds, some ten years before, The Club had been a predominantly literary institution with Samuel Johnson and Oliver Goldsmith among its more distinguished frequenters. But as the years passed, its membership began subtly to change, scientists being admitted as well as the literary men, critics, and dramatists who had attended its meetings in the past. England was changing, too. In the country men and women were beginning to leave the handlooms in their cottages to sit at wooden machines in workshops; towns were slowly growing; windmills and watermills were disappearing and tall chimneys were pouring forth a thick black smoke over the surrounding fields. Within twenty years of Dr Johnson's death, William Blake was writing of the 'dark, satanic mills' whose high brick walls were the prisons of the poor. By the time of

Blake's death in 1827, James Hargreaves had invented the spinning frame which he named after his wife, Jenny; Richard Arkwright had set up his own spinning machines in his large factory in Derbyshire; Henry Cort had revolutionized the manufacture of iron; Edmund Cartwright had invented the power-loom; James Watt's steam engines were grinding malt in Whitbread's Brewery; Richard Trevithick's steam-carriage had run between Leather Lane and Paddington, and George Stephenson was experimenting with the locomotives which were to culminate in the *Rocket*, capable of racing along at thirty miles an hour.

A steam engine perfected by the Cornish engineer, Richard Trevithick, in 1808.

Pioneered by the Duke of Bridgewater, whose waterway between his coalmines at Worsley and Manchester was opened in 1761, canals were being dug by armies of men known as navigators or navvies all over the country where they still form a network of inland waterways from the Grand Union Canal and the Grand Junction Canal to the Ellesmere and Manchester Ship Canals at whose junction at Ellesmere Port is the Boat Museum where some of the ships that used to carry goods on them are preserved. Before the century was over there was not a large town in England which was not on a canal or within fifteen miles of one, some towns owing their very existence to the new waterways. Stourport in Worcestershire, for example – a town of some 4,500 inhabitants with ironworks, carpet-weaving factories and tanneries – had been developed because of the importance of its site at the junction of the Stour, the Severn and the Staffordshire and Worcester Canal.

Road transport was also being transformed: John McAdam, a magistrate and road trustee born in Scotland in 1756, had introduced new methods of drainage and surfacing; turnpike trusts, of which there were over nine hundred by the 1830s, had improved thousands of miles of roads by the erection of gates and bars and the collection of tolls by keepers, many of whose little houses, such as the one at Folly Bridge in Oxford, are still in existence; and hundreds of bridges had been built. Among the most remarkable of

Vase from the workshop of Josiah Wedgwood, modelled upon a Roman original.

these were the world's first iron bridge built in 1779 by the ironmaster, Abraham Darby, across the Severn in Shropshire at the place known as Ironbridge – where several museums vividly re-create the area's industrial past – and the Menai Suspension Bridge built by the Scottish engineer, Thomas Telford, in 1825. This was the forerunner of the Clifton Suspension Bridge planned in 1829-31 by Isambard Kingdom Brunel, designer of the Great Britain, the first ocean-going steamer with screw propulsion, which now lies in dock at Bristol.

Many of those travelling across these new bridges had little notion of the miserable lives led in the slums and factories of the growing towns. There were, to be sure, factories where the conditions of work were considered exemplary. For instance in that gloomy area of the Midlands known as the Black Country – where the restored bottle kilns of the Gladstone Pottery Museum at Longton provide a vivid impression of the work once undertaken there – Josiah Wedgwood's employees lived under their master's firm paternalistic care in a model village, Etruria, which had been especially built for them. And in Birmingham, whose population had risen from about 12,000 at the beginning of the 18th century to 45,000 in 1800, an American visitor to one of the town's factories found 'no mark of ill-humour' among the hundreds of persons employed there. Yet there were other places, factories, mines and sweatshops, where the conditions were appalling, where children were employed as well as women and were pushed into tubs of cold water to keep them awake during their interminable hours of labour.

In the earlier years of the nineteenth century there were protests and uprisings, riots against the Corn Laws – which had been passed by Parliament in 1815 to protect British agriculture and maintain the level of rents by charging high duties on imported grain – and demonstrations against the savage punishments imposed upon machine-breakers whose activities, it was feared for a time, might provoke a national revolution. In 1819 in St Peter's Field, Manchester, a large crowd of people, many of them distressed handloom weavers attending a rally in support of parliamentary reform, were charged by mounted troops who killed eleven of them and wounded hundreds more in what became known as the Peterloo Massacre in ironic allusion to the battle of Waterloo. In 1820 a group of radicals meeting in a stable loft in Cato Street conspired to murder the entire Cabinet while they were having dinner and to carry off the heads of the Home and Foreign Secretaries in bags. Betrayed to the authorities, five of the ringleaders were hanged. They were spared being drawn and quartered because of public sympathy; but even so the hangman was attacked in the street and almost castrated. Ten years later, in protests against low wages and farm machinery, there were serious riots all over England as gangs of men with blackened faces, sometimes in women's clothes and often carrying flags and blowing horns, cut down fences, destroyed machinery and burnt down ricks and barns. Men who declined to join in the rioting were thrown into village ponds; and parties of yeomanry called out to suppress it were attacked with pick-axes and hatchets. When the risings were at last brought under control, several rioters had been hanged, well over 600 sent to prison and 500 sentenced to transportation, nearly all to the Australian colonies. Soon afterwards, in 1834, in the Dorset village of Tolpuddle, six farm labourers who had administered oaths to their fellow workers were arrested and charged with having administered 'illegal' oaths for 'seditious' purposes. Although trade unions had been legalized ten years before, the men from Tolpuddle were arraigned under an eighteenth-century Mutiny Act and, like the rick-burning rioters, were sentenced to transportation.

The furious protests which these punishments aroused could not be ignored, however; and it was clear that a new age, later to be known as the Age of Reform, had begun.

'The Peterloo Massacre' of 1819 in Manchester where several demonstrators were killed by yeomanry.

Todmorden, Yorkshire, a typical Victorian industrial landscape.

'It was only yesterday,' exclaims one of Thackeray's characters, 'but what a gulf between now and then. *Then* was the old world. Stage-coaches, more or less swift riding horses, packhorses, highwaymen ... But your railroad starts a new era ... We who lived before railways and survive out of the ancient world, are like Father Noah and his family out of the Ark.'

Certainly, since the opening in 1825 of the first public railway, the Stockton and Darlington, the whole tenor of English life as well as the English landscape had been transformed. By 1852 there were only a few market towns and coastal resorts without a railway station; twenty years later all these had been provided with one. By 1875 nearly five hundred million passengers were being transported each year, and all London's main termini, except Blackfriars (1886) and Marylebone (1899), had been completed. Some were horrified by the change the railways brought about. The Duke of Wellington, who survived until 1852, complained that 'people never acted so foolishly as we did in allowing for the Destruction of our excellent and commodious [post roads] in order to expend Millions Sterling on these Rail Roads ... the vulgarest, most indelicate, most injurious to Health of any mode of conveyance' that he had seen in any part of the world. Yet there were advantages as well as regrets. The railways helped the new towns to grow, and as they grew, so did the capacity of their inhabitants to

An early Victorian steam train emerging from a tunnel near Bath on the Great Western Railway.

enjoy fresh food: the sponsors of the London to Birmingham line's London terminus at Euston noted with pride that it was built on the site of a warren of cowsheds and cow-cellars from which the nearby households had previously been supplied with tainted and watered milk instead of the fresh milk that could now be brought in from the country. Moreover, as it became possible for people to travel beyond the confines of the enclosed communities they had rarely been able to escape before, they discarded their previous suspicions of the outside world and learned both that their fellow countrymen were much like themselves and that social justice, as the reformers encouraged men and women to think, was a national concern.

Among these reformers was William Cobbett, who died in 1835. A farmer's son and former sergeant-major, whose *Rural Rides* is a vivid and revealing portrait of England in the early nineteenth century, Cobbett had become one of the most influential of the anti-establishment radicals. His contemporary, Jeremy Bentham, a leading proponent of parliamentary reform, had found wide support for his belief that legislation must aim to achieve 'the greatest happiness of the greatest number'; and Robert Owen, the Welsh social reformer whose sympathetic management of the New Lanark cotton-mills had induced other owners to introduce

Mill workers in New Lanark where Robert Owen had founded his model industrial environment in 1800-29.

Sir Robert Peel, Home Secretary from 1822 and Prime Minister, 1834-5 and 1841-6.

more enlightened methods into their own concerns, had strenuously supported the Factory Act of 1819 which gave a measure of protection to children employed in industry. Thereafter the pace of reform had begun hesitantly to quicken. As Home Secretary from 1822, Robert Peel had introduced a series of measures lessening the severity of the criminal law, which as late as 1819 had still recognized as many as 223 offences as punishable by death; and in 1829 he saw the Metropolitan Police Bill, which proposed the creation of the capital's first professional police force, pass both Houses without serious opposition, paving the way for a paid constabulary in all the counties of England. In 1829 Roman Catholics were at last granted full civil and political rights by the Roman Catholic Emancipation Act. And, at the general election of 1830, the Whigs under Lord Grey were returned to power after more than half a century in opposition and turned their minds to the problem of parliamentary reform.

Although the Tories were traditionally opposed to the measure, it had long been generally conceded that parliamentary reform was overdue. Only about one person in every hundred had a vote; and, while several large towns such as Manchester – whose population with that of Salford had already risen to 84,000 by 1801 – had no representative in Parliament at all, there were several places far smaller which had two. There were also various so-called rotten or pocket boroughs, like Satton which was no more than a park and Dunwich which had for centuries been submerged beneath the North Sea. These were mostly in the hands of landowners who nominated Members as they chose. George Selwyn, for example, the rich and witty Member for Gloucester who would travel anywhere to watch a good hanging, owned the pocket borough of Luggershall in Wiltshire. He agreed to sell it to General Simon Fraser when it seemed that Fraser, who was standing for Inverness-shire, might be defeated by his opponent, Lord George Gordon.

Fraser consulted his father, Lord Lovat, who in turn spoke to the Duke of Gordon, Lord George's elder brother. Between them they decided it would be cheaper to buy Selwyn's seat than to bribe all the electors of Inverness-shire. So Luggershall was bought and presented to Lord George Gordon who accordingly agreed to withdraw from Inverness-shire so as to leave the field clear for Simon Fraser. Nobody regarded the transaction as anything out of the ordinary.

It was in order to prevent such deals by the abolition of rotten boroughs, to grant seats to new towns which lacked them and to give the vote to certain additional holders of property that Lord Grey's government brought forward their modest Reform Bill in 1831. The member of the government mainly responsible for drafting the Bill was Lord John Russell, son of the 6th Duke of Bedford, a clever and persuasive little man whose heart was set on reform both political and educational. Despite a persuasive speech by Russell in the Commons, the Bill was defeated. Grey therefore resigned and appealed to the country; the Whigs were returned again with a large majority; and the Bill, somewhat amended, was again presented to the Commons who now passed it. The government could not, however, get it through the Lords; and it was not until Lord Grey went to see the King, George IV's brother William IV, that the problem was resolved. Grey proposed that the King should create a sufficient number of new peers to ensure the passage of the Bill. The King, naturally reluctant to do so – since such a measure would threaten the whole fabric of the Upper House – was saved from the necessity by the Tories' submission. Their leader, the Duke of Wellington, advised acceptance of the Bill which eventually became law in May 1832.

The next year a whole series of reforms were enacted. Many of them were proposed by the 7th Earl of Shaftesbury, the indefatigable philanthropist in whose memory was erected the statue by Alfred Gilbert known as Eros at Piccadilly Circus and after whom Shaftesbury Avenue was

William IV succeeded his brother George IV in 1830 to be faced with the constitutional problems posed by the Reform Bill.

A boy working in a colliery in Northumberland.

named. Shaftesbury concerned himself with a wide variety of causes, from the plight of lunatics to the laws relating to the employment of women and children in factories and mines, from the treatment of chimney sweepers' climbing-boys to the education of the poor and the eradication of slums. It was, indeed, largely due to Shaftesbury's efforts that some of the worst abuses in society were brought to the attention of a generally complacent middle class.

While Shaftesbury was concerning himself with the plight of the English poor, other reformers were struggling to abolish slavery and to complete the work of William Wilberforce, the rich merchant's son and close friend of Pitt, who had done so much to kill the slave trade itself in 1807. Their efforts met with success in 1833 when – in the year that Shaftesbury's Factory Act made it illegal to employ children below the age of thirteen for more than 48 hours a week – slavery was abolished throughout the British Empire.

Much as was achieved by Lord Grey's government and those of his successors, Melbourne and Peel, radicals had cause to complain that progress was not proceeding fast enough and that some innovations were positively deleterious. The Mines and Collieries Act of 1842, it was admitted, went some way towards dealing with the exploitation of

A chimney sweep's trade card.

164

women and children in coal mines by prohibiting the employment of women underground as well as boys under ten. But the Poor Law Amendment Act of 1834 did little to ameliorate the miseries of the destitute. Before the passing of this Act, poor relief had been administered by the system known as the Speenhamland System from the place in Berkshire where the justices had originally devised it. By this method exceptionally low wages had been supplemented from parish rates, a system which, far from relieving poverty, encouraged employers to keep wages low. The Poor Law which abolished it, however, instead of offering relief to paupers, by giving them sufficient money to survive in their own homes, forced them into workhouses, and was far from an agreeable alternative, since conditions in workhouses were deliberately rendered so unpleasant that most poor people did all they could to avoid entering them. Charles Dickens's description of workhouse fare as constituting 'three meals of thin gruel a day, with an onion twice a week, and half a roll on Sundays' – while not intended to be taken as exact – was not far from the truth; and the bowl of soup and small piece of bread which the poor boys are given in the large stone hall in *Oliver Twist* was not an unusual meal under a system by which children under nine years of age were dieted 'at discretion'.

A beggar woman photographed in London in 1875.

There was widespread dissatisfaction with the new Poor Law and with the Reform Act which, while welcomed by the propertied middle classes, was a profound disappointment to radicals and the militant working class. There was dissatisfaction also with the failure of attempts to develop trade unionism; and this general discontent ensured that unrest continued throughout the 1830s and helped to increase support for the movement for political reform known as Chartism.

This movement took its name from a People's Charter drawn up in 1838 by a group of radicals who demanded of the government universal male suffrage and vote by secret ballot, equal electoral districts, annual parliaments, an end to property qualifications for Members of Parliament, and the introduction of salaries for them. Support for these six demands was loudly voiced at meetings held both by day and night all over the country. One such gathering at Halifax attracted a crowd of 200,000. 'It is almost impossible to imagine the excitement caused,' one Chartist wrote of these rallies. 'Working people met in their thousands and tens of thousands to swear devotion to the common cause ... The processions were frequently of immense length ... The meetings themselves were of a still more terrific character.' In 1839 there was a threat of a general strike; and later on that year when 7,000 men, mostly miners and iron-workers, marched through the streets of Newport, Monmouthshire, demanding the release of a Chartist orator from the local gaol, soldiers opened fire on them and at least twenty-two were killed.

There were riots, too, in renewed protest against the Corn Laws whose effects were exacerbated by a series of poor harvests. In 1839 an Anti-Corn Law League was founded to denounce the Laws as benefiting landowners at the expense of workers; and speakers propounding the views of the League, and raising funds for its propaganda, travelled all over the country in the steps of Richard Cobden, a Sussex farmer's son who, in his own words, 'lived in public meetings', and John Bright, the son of a Quaker mill owner from Lancashire. In the opinion of a Tory landlord, expressing a general view, the League was 'the most cunning, unscrupulous, knavish, pestilent body of men that ever plagued this or any other country.' But it was a Tory Prime Minister, Robert Peel, who, after a poor harvest in England and the failure of the potato crop in Ireland, was persuaded in 1846 that the Corn Law must be repealed. The decision came too late. In Ireland, where potatoes were the staple diet, about a million people perished of starvation or disease and a further million emigrated, many of them to America where they nurtured a hatred of England shared by most of the Irish people who remained behind. The decision split the Tory party. Although he steered the repeal through Parliament, Peel was obliged to resign, and many of his followers joined the Whigs – now the developing Liberal Party soon to be dominated by the towering figure of William Ewart Gladstone – while the remaining Tories, or Conservatives as they were now more generally known, regrouped themselves under Benjamin Disraeli, a Christianized Jew of mixed Italian and Spanish descent who had attacked the government's proposal to repeal the Corn Laws in a series of brilliant speeches. Disraeli poured such scorn upon Peel that his victim, a shy, awkward man with an aloof manner and an excessive sensitivity to ridicule, was observed more than once to change colour dramatically as he listened, to laugh loudly and defensively in pretence of amusement, or to pull his hat down over his eyes and his nervously twitching face.

W.E. Gladstone, the Grand Old Man of liberal politics, became Prime Minister for the first time in 1868.

Upon Peel's resignation in 1846, the Liberal Lord John Russell became Prime Minister; and it was his government which had to deal with the continuing problems presented by the Chartists who were planning to organize a massive demonstration in London and to present a petition to Parliament containing even more signatures than the three million appended to an earlier petition of 1842. The demonstration was planned for 1848, the year of revolutions on the Continent where the King of France was forced to abdicate and the Austrian Empire and Germany were both in uproar. It was hoped by the Chartist leaders that revolution might break out in England, too. The Royal Family were advised to leave London for the safety of their house at Osborne on the Isle of Wight. Already the lamps outside Buckingham Palace had been smashed and shouts of '*Vive la république!*' had been heard. But Lord John Russell's government, of which the pugnacious Lord Palmerston was a senior member, stood firm. Immense numbers of police were brought into London; 150,000 special constables were enrolled; yeomanry regiments were called up. Feargus O'Connor, the Irish orator and journalist, a leading figure in the Chartist movement, urged the crowds to disperse. Another Chartist leader gloomily conceded that the government had proved too strong for the workers. Thereafter Chartism gradually declined. And Queen Victoria, in tears and shivering with fright before she left for Osborne, expressed her profound relief that the trouble was over, that the workmen, misled by professional agitators and the 'criminals and refuse of London', remained loyal after all.

Queen Victoria, who had succeeded her uncle, William IV, in 1837, was then twenty-nine years old, the mother of six children and the happy wife of Prince Albert of Saxe-Coburg and Gotha whom she manifestly adored. Although well instructed in her rights and duties by her first Prime Minister, Lord Melbourne, the Queen was not content to be a mere figurehead and interfered in the processes of government far more insistently than her ministers thought seeming or the constitution allowed. An emotional and selfish woman, difficult, demanding and capricious, she was imperious, though innately shy, finding throughout her life official engagements unusually tiring as they not only bored her but made her nervous. Often she had to restrain herself from giggling. She had little cause, however, to be unsure of herself in the presence of ministers, for she had many varied talents of her own. Her intellect was limited, but she had an astonishingly good memory. She was hardworking, well-informed and shrewd. Her judgements, however, were never tentative, never in doubt. Incapable of lying or dissembling herself, she was also incapable of understanding that there were degrees of reprehensibility. A thing was right or it was wrong; a person was good or bad; and, once her mind was made up, she had absolute confidence in her opinion. She played the part of Queen and Empress with an instinctive and formidable distinction.

The monarch had, and has, every constitutional right to make suggestions; yet Queen Victoria often overstepped the limits of constitutional propriety, writing to her royal relations on political matters without the knowledge of the

The world's first adhesive postage stamp, the 'penny black', introduced on 6 May 1840.

Cabinet, corresponding with generals without reference to the War Minister, and with former Prime Ministers behind the backs of their successors, threatening to abdicate if the government pursued policies of which she disapproved, on occasions actively supporting and encouraging the opposition, and reacting angrily at any hint of criticism. Although Prince Albert is justly given credit for helping to guide the Queen towards the creation of a new English monarchical tradition which placed the throne above party, he, too, was prone to the kind of constitutional indiscretion encouraged by his adviser, Baron Stockmar, who was of the dangerous opinion that the monarch was the 'permanent Premier' and the Prime Minister merely 'the temporary head of the Cabinet'.

Although never much liked in the country at large, Prince Albert was generally respected by the Queen's ministers; and after his premature death, which laid her prostrate with grief, it was considered only appropriate that his memory should be honoured by the Albert Memorial in Kensington Gardens, the highly expensive monument in which the statue of the Prince is seen holding the catalogue of the Great Exhibition of 1851 which he had done so much to organize and encourage.

The Great Exhibition of over 100,000 objects from all over the world was held in a specially constructed Crystal Palace designed by Joseph Paxton on the lines of a conservatory he had created for the Duke of Devonshire at Chatsworth in Derbyshire. The Crystal Palace was afterwards removed to Sydenham where it served as the first home of the Imperial War Museum whose new premises – part of the old Bethlem Royal Hospital in Lambeth – now contain a model of the original Palace burned down in 1936. The Exhibition held here in 1851 was a notable success, attracting over six million visitors and making a handsome profit which, with the help of funds voted by Parliament, paid for the transformation of a large part of Kensington where Exhibition Road, Queen's Gate and

Cromwell Road – all names chosen by Prince Albert himself – were built soon afterwards. Also built on land purchased by the Great Exhibition Commissioners in the 1850s were the Albert Hall, the Victoria and Albert Museum, the Natural History Museum, the Science Museum, and the Geological Museum.

At the same time the University Museum was built in Oxford. At the strong instigation of John Ruskin, whose *Stones of Venice* was published in 1851-3, this museum was built in the Gothic style, the style chosen also for the Houses of Parliament, rebuilt after their destruction by fire in 1834. Thereafter Gothic was selected for numerous churches, country houses and collegiate buildings throughout the country, from G. E. Street's Royal Courts of Justice in the Strand and William Butterfield's Keble College, Oxford to Alfred Waterhouse's Manchester Town Hall and George Gilbert Scott's Midland Hotel, St Pancras Station.

When in 1831 work had begun on the huge Gothic Harlaxton Manor in Lincolnshire to the designs of Anthony Salvin and its owner Gregory Gregory, there had been little enthusiasm for this style. The architect of the Gothic Houses of Parliament, Charles Barry, would have preferred to have submitted a Renaissance design; and when in the

The Houses of Parliament under construction after the destruction of the earlier Palace of Westminster by fire in 1834.

1860s new government offices were required along Whitehall Lord Palmerston received vociferous support when he insisted that they should be in Italianate rather than in the Gothic style, which Sir George Gilbert Scott at first proposed. But by the time Ruskin had resigned his Professorship of Fine Arts at Oxford in 1884 and retired to the seclusion of Brantwood he had succeeded in changing a whole generation's attitude to architecture. Despite the outrageous prejudice of some of his statements, he had ultimately convinced most of his countrymen that the Gothic style which he had so passionately championed – and which was so grandly exploited for the creation of Allerton Park, North Yorkshire – was a style far better suited than any other to reflect the glories of the British past. By his defence of J. M. W. Turner, whose work was at first derided by the critics, Ruskin had also taught the public to recognize the genius of the most original landscape painter of the nineteenth century; while by his advocacy of Holman Hunt, Millais, Rossetti and the other Pre-Raphaelites, he had encouraged a revolt against the conventional academic painting of the day.

A social reformer, as well as author and artist, Ruskin concerned himself also with national education, the organization of labour, the foundation of training schools, old-age pensions, and the building of decent homes for the working class. Moreover he supported the kind of industrial experiments advocated by William Morris whose revival of handicrafts and views of house decoration, as exemplified by the decorations and furniture in his own houses – the Red House in Bexleyheath, Kent, Kelmscott House, Hammersmith and Kelmscott in Oxfordshire – were revolutionizing English taste.

Many of Ruskin's reformist ideas were ridiculed in his time and dismissed out of hand by successive governments. Lord Palmerston, who was brought to power when the Conservative government of Lord Aberdeen revealed its incompetence during the Crimean War against Russia in

The Natural History Museum, one of several museums erected in South Kensington after the Great Exhibition, designed by Alfred Waterhouse and opened in 1881.

Kelmscott Manor in Oxfordshire where William Morris lived from 1871 until his death in 1896.

Queen Victoria with her 'kindest and most devoted minister', Benjamin Disraeli, Earl of Beaconsfield.

1854-6, was for most of his time in office preoccupied with foreign affairs, with the suppression of the mutiny of the native soldiers of the Indian army in 1857, with the problems presented by the struggles for the unification of Italy and with the conflicts precipitated by the opium trade in China – a trade which a Parliamentary Committee had deemed it 'inadvisable to abandon since it engendered so important a revenue'. Britain's overseas possessions, of which the Queen was so proud and which covered so many thousands of square miles marked in pink on the maps of schoolroom walls, were still, after all, widely regarded as being held to serve the business interests of British merchants and manufacturers and to provide the mother country with raw materials, even though, since the loss of the American colonies, there had grown up a new conception of Empire as being not merely a means to riches through trade but a political organization of peoples involving responsibilities as well as rights.

From 1867, however, when Disraeli – who became Conservative Prime Minister for the first time the next year – was largely instrumental in pushing through the second Reform Act, which almost doubled the electorate, until 1894 when his rival, Gladstone, retired at the age of 84, the pace of reform, much of it inspired by the writings of J. S. Mill, equalled that of the Shaftesbury era. The Education Act of 1870 introduced universal elementary education; the Trade Union Act of 1871 gave unions legal status and a later Act the right to picket peacefully; the Ballot Act of 1872 made voting secret, putting an end to bribery and intimidation. Long overdue reforms were instituted in the Army by Edward Cardwell as Secretary for War from 1868 to 1874; in public health by Sir Edwin Chadwick; and in hospital administration by Florence Nightingale, who having trained in Prussia and France, had gone out to nurse the sick and wounded and badger the medical department in the dreadful hospitals of the Crimea. There were reforms also in land tenure and poor relief; in the constitution of the

One of numerous commemorative mugs made in Queen Victoria's reign.

The 1879 Battle of Isandhlwana where the Zulus annihilated a British force.

universities and in the treatment of prisoners.

From time to time the attention of the public was diverted from this erratic march of progress by the outbreak of wars and the progress of events in the now huge British Empire. There was intermittent fighting along the frontiers of India whose imperial crown the Queen assumed in 1876; there was fighting in Afghanistan after the assassination of the British Resident in Kabul; there was trouble, too, in Egypt from whose bankrupt Khedive Disraeli bought a controlling interest in the Suez Canal on behalf of the government and presented the shares to the Queen, as though they were a personal gift, with the words, 'You have it, madam, the entire interest of the Khedive is now yours.' There was fighting in the Sudan where General Gordon perished attempting to evacuate Egyptian forces from Khartoum and Kitchener at last established British authority by his victory at Omdurman. In Zululand a British force was destroyed at Isandhlwana; in South Africa peace came only after further humiliating defeats at the hands of the Dutch settlers, the Boers, had been revenged by General Roberts. And, as always, there was trouble in Ireland.

By the 1880s Gladstone had come to the conclusion that the demands for Irish Home Rule, that is to say, for an Irish parliament responsible for the island's domestic affairs,

Charles Stuart Parnell, the Irish nationalist whose career was ruined after he had been cited in a divorce case.

made by Charles Stewart Parnell and other Irish Members of Parliament, must be met. The Queen was horrified, writing to the Prince of Wales to express her dissatisfaction with her 'dreadfully Radical Government ... and the way in which they truckled to the Home Rulers – as well as the utter disregard of all my opinions which after 45 years of experience ought to be considered.' She had never liked or trusted the Irish; and Gladstone's suggestion that she should spend as much time there as she did at her beloved Scottish home, Balmoral, was an absurd idea, just such a one as might have been expected from this 'wild incomprehensible ... half-mad firebrand'. If only Disraeli had lived all would have been different. But Disraeli had died in 1881 and now lay buried in the village churchyard near his country house at Hughenden.

Had he and his party wished it, Disraeli might have persuaded the Queen to regard Home Rule with less hostility. By his ingratiating tact and fulsome flattery, by the impression he gave of needing to consult her and have the advice of her astute mind, he contrived on occasions to change it. He recognized himself that he often 'laid it on rather thick' with his coaxing blandishments. But, as he said to Matthew Arnold, 'You have heard me called a flatterer, and it is true. Everyone likes flattery; and when you come to royalty, you should lay it on with a trowel.' But he never underestimated the Queen's astuteness; he grew genuinely fond of her – even though he declined to see her when he was dying on the grounds that she would only want him to take a message to Albert – and, in treating her with elaborate courtesy, he was behaving towards her as he did to all women he liked. Gladstone, a man of the utmost moral rectitude who hated dissembling, could not bring himself to treat the Queen in such a way. He addressed her, so she said, as though she were a public meeting and was quite incapable of following the advice of his wife who sensibly said to him, 'Do pet the Queen, and for once believe you can, you dear old thing.' But it was not in Gladstone's nature to do so. He was a man of remarkable political and administrative ability as well as a splendid and powerful orator. There was great nobility in his character; yet there was in his manner something of the pious humbug. In a telling comment the Liberal politician and journalist, Henry Labouchère, said of him that he did not object to Gladstone 'always having the ace of trumps up his sleeve, but only to his pretence that God had put it there'. It was to this aspect of Gladstone's character that the Queen took exception; and when his Home Rule Bill was defeated by a combination of Conservatives and dissidents in his own party, the Queen accepted his resignation, and the Marquess of Salisbury as his Conservative successor, with unconcealed satisfaction. Upon Gladstone's death in 1898 she declined to express any grief. 'No, I did not like the man,' she declared with characteristic honesty. 'How can I say I am sorry when I am not?' It was left to her eldest son to pay the widow due respects: he kissed Mrs Gladstone's hand at the funeral and, to his mother's annoyance, played the part of pall-bearer. Three years later the Queen, too, was dead; and the age to which she had given a name died with her.

The term Victorian was already in use in 1875 when Victoria had over a quarter of a century to live. It has been taken to imply a regard for hard work and thrift, strict morality and family virtues; in one dictionary it is defined as 'exhibiting the characteristics popularly attributed to the Victorians, especially prudery, bigotry or hypocrisy'.

The Queen's eldest son, with whom she had so often found fault, and who now succeeded her as Edward VII, was unarguably a Victorian by birth but very far from being a Victorian by nature. He seemed, indeed, a highly appropriate figure to preside over the society that drifted – as apparently unconcerned as the *Titanic* steaming towards the icebergs of the north Atlantic – into war with the Germany of the nephew whom he so much disliked, Kaiser Wilhelm II.

Four generations of the Royal Family, Queen Victoria with the future Edward VII (right), George V (left), and Edward VIII in a sailor suit.

1901 – 1990 **THE TWENTIETH CENTURY**

King George V, who was trained in the Royal Navy, racing the cutter *Britannia*, which he inherited upon his father's death in 1910.

Previous page:
St Paul's Cathedral in the Blitz.

Night life in Edwardian London.

The King who came to the throne in 1901 and who gave his name to the Edwardian era, is remembered for none of the staid Victorian virtues which might have been expected from a man born in 1841 but rather for his self-indulgence and extravagance, his enormous girth and gruff *bonhomie*, his fondness for good and expensive food, fast horses, pretty women, huge cigars, France and shooting on his Norfolk estate at Sandringham. His short reign, to quote R. J. White, 'lingers on the edge of subsequent darkness like a long summer afternoon, quietly punctuated by the popping of champagne corks, flavoured with cigar smoke, and accompanied by the distant strains of Elgar's *Pomp and Circumstance* march from the Guards' Band in the Park.'

For many English people life in the years before the First World War was far from that associated with visions of *la belle époque*. Beneath the glittering surface of society there was widespread poverty, bitterness and unrest. Yet year by year, by slow degrees, reforms continued to come and the quality of life for the mass of the people gradually improved, with advances undreamed of a century before in medicine and housing, in technology and conditions of work. Farming emerged from the agricultural depression of the 1870s and 1880s; and in the towns successful strikes were organized by the poorly paid and the exploited. Striking dockers, for example, were promised the modest wage of sixpence an hour which they had demanded; and when the match-girls at Bryant and May's factory went on strike in 1888 against the dangerous, ill-paid and squalid conditions of their work they won their case. In that year a Local Government Act established county councils; in subsequent years factory acts made further improvements in conditions of work, housing acts eliminated some of the worst slums, and education acts brought free schools and free school meals within the reach of thousands of poor children. For the better-off scores of independent schools were founded to instil in their pupils those 'religious and moral principles' and 'manly conduct' which Dr Arnold had required of his boys at Rugby, one of those numerous so-called public schools, many of them founded in the previous century, whose role in turning boys into gentlemen was seen by their critics as one of the main foundations upon which the indestructible English class system was based.

There were still those who agreed with the physician, Sir Almroth Wright, that 'there are no good women, but only women who have lived under the influence of good men'; but there were far more who recognized that women had lived for far too long with as few rights and as little freedom as the 'doll in the doll's house' which Bella Rokesmith complains of being in *Our Mutual Friend* or as Sally Brass's downtrodden maid in *The Old Curiosity Shop* who is 'ignorant of the taste of beer, unacquainted with her own name (which is less remarkable) and [takes] a limited view of life through the keyhole of doors'. In the field of medicine, for example, after the admittance of Elizabeth Garrett Anderson to the Medical Register in 1865, and the establishment of the London School of Medicine for Women in 1876, the infiltration of women into what had previously been regarded as a male preserve was generally accepted. In 1882 a Women's Property Act at last enabled married women to own their own property; and while the militant feminist movement of the Suffragettes, the demonstrations and strikes of Mrs Pankhurst's Women's Social and Political Union, and such desperate protests as that of Emily Davison who threw herself beneath the King's horse at the Derby in 1913, were brought to an end by the War, votes were granted to women over thirty as soon as the fighting was over and to all women on the same terms as men ten years later.

In 1905 a general election brought the Liberals back to power under Sir Henry Campbell-Bannerman whose Cabinet included H. H. Asquith, the son of a Nonconformist wool-spinner from Lancashire, David Lloyd George, whose mother was the poor widow of a Welsh schoolmaster, and Winston Churchill, grandson of the 7th Duke of Marlborough, all three of whom were to be

Mrs Emmeline Pankhurst, arrested outside Buckingham Palace in May 1914.

Poster of 1910 protesting against the Welsh Lloyd George and his 'socialist budget'.

prime ministers in their turn.

Campbell-Bannerman's government occupied themselves earnestly with reform, as did that of his successor, Asquith. More slums were cleared and towns replanned; labour exchanges were established and minimum wages fixed in certain industries; pensions were paid to the old; and, by the Trade Disputes Act of 1906, unions were granted protection from liability for losses caused by strikes. The Lords had looked askance at several of these Liberal measures without actually blocking them. But when Lloyd George, as Chancellor of the Exchequer – in an attempt to raise money for his government's reforms, as well as for rearmament against Germany – brought in his budget in 1909 proposing higher death duties as well as a land tax and a supertax on incomes over £3,000 a year, they rebelled. And it was not until after two general elections had been fought, and Edward VII's son, King George V, had been prevailed upon to agree to the creation if necessary of over 200 Liberal peers to outvote the Conservatives that the crisis was resolved. In 1911 the Parliament Act was passed, severely curtailing the powers of the Lords and establishing the Commons as the supreme legislative body. In that same year a National Insurance Act provided relief for the sick and the unemployed; and a salary of £400 was introduced for Members of Parliament who, soon after-wards, included men supported as candidates by trade unions. Already James Keir Hardie, a former miner and Secretary of the Scottish Miners' Federation, had become leader of the Independent Labour Party, forerunner of a Labour Party dedicated to a socialist policy of 'common ownership of the means of production'; and Ramsay MacDonald, also Scottish, the illegitimate child of a maid-servant and a ploughman, and one day to be the first Labour Prime Minister, had been elected to Parliament as Member for Leicester.

The problem of Ireland remained unresolved and appar-ently insoluble. After the failure of a second Home Rule Bill, relations between the Irish nationalists and the Protestants of Ulster, who were determined not to lose their identity in a Roman Catholic Ireland, went from bad to worse until the Government of Ireland Act proposed parti-tion with separate parliaments for north-east and south. This solution provoked such resistance in the south that its 26 counties had eventually to be granted virtual indepen-dence from Britain, with the six counties of the north-east remaining part of the United Kingdom. This proved unac-ceptable to the Irish Republican Army and its supporters who demanded, and still demand, the withdrawal of British troops from Ulster and the establishment of a republic of the whole of Ireland.

A recruiting poster of the First World War.

Despite the quarrels, thousands of Irishmen joined the British Army when Britain declared war on Germany in August 1914 after the Kaiser's troops had invaded Belgium; and by November 1918, when the dreadful struggle was over, there were many Irish corpses among the million British dead. Lloyd George, who had replaced Asquith as Prime Minister at the height of the conflict, promised the survivors that he would undertake 'to make Britain a fit country for heroes to live in'. For a time it appeared that this promise might be fulfilled. But the post-war boom was over

181

within two years and was followed by a long period of depression, strikes and hunger marches. By 1921 there were over two million unemployed. The next year Lloyd George was obliged to resign, never to return to office, and to witness the eclipse of the Liberals by the Labour Party as the main opposition to the Conservatives. He was succeeded by the Conservatives under Bonar Law, followed by Stanley Baldwin, a square-faced, pipe-smoking, seemingly lethargic man, then by a Labour government under Ramsay MacDonald, then in 1924 by Baldwin again.

In 1926 a General Strike was called in support of the miners who, after its failure, were forced by hunger to return to work with longer hours and lower wages even than before. Yet, outside the mining districts, the strike seemed to have improved rather than worsened relations between the poor workers and the well-to-do, the 'two nations' into which Disraeli had described the country as being divided in the previous century. The middle classes who had volunteered to take the place of strikers to keep essential services running had, for the first time, come to understand the nature of manual work and to respect those who undertook it, while the workers, brought into contact with people whose backgrounds were so different from

George V and his cabinet in 1920, including Stanley Baldwin (back row, left), Lord Curzon (front row, left), David Lloyd George (on the King's right) and Austen Chamberlain (far right).

their own, were surprised to discover how much in common they shared.

It was an opportunity for the 'lasting peace' for which the King called. But, although Baldwin, too, was a moderate man, pressing always for conciliation rather than confrontation, the opportunity was lost. Legislation was imposed upon the unions that much reduced their powers; and largely as a result of their repressive measures, the Conservatives lost their majority and had to give way in 1929 to another Labour government which, after the American slump, was faced with an economy close to collapse and three million unemployed. After disagreements in the Cabinet over cuts in unemployment benefit, this beleaguered Labour government felt obliged to form a coalition government with the Conservatives and Liberals in 1931.

Unless they happened to come across some such 'hunger march' as that of the unemployed shipyard workers who came down to London in 1936 from Jarrow in Durham – where two-thirds of the population was out of work – visitors to the south of England found it hard to believe that the country was faced with any kind of crisis, financial or otherwise. For this was the world of the cocktail and the slow fox trot, of Noël Coward's *Hay Fever*, of Somerset Maugham's *The Constant Wife*, of Sapper's *Bull-Dog Drummond* and Michael Arlen's *The Green Hat*, as well as that of the economist, John Maynard Keynes, and of the socialist, Harold Laski, of Kingsley Martin's *New Statesman*, of G. B. Shaw's *Intelligent Woman's Guide to Socialism and Capitalism*, and of T. S. Eliot and W. H. Auden. It was the day of the motor car – there were already two million of them on the roads by 1939 – and the age of the seaside holiday: Blackpool alone had seven million visitors a year.

The architecture of the period reflected its mood. Scores of hotels were being built like the Park Lane and the Mayfair, both completed in 1927, the Strand Palace of 1930 and the Dorchester of 1931. Hundreds of cinemas

Shipyard workers march to London from Jarrow to protest against unemployment in the North East.

An advertisement of 1933 for Morris Motors.

183

A cinema queue in 1934.

A 1908 London Underground poster advertising the pleasures of suburban life in Golders Green.

at the same time, from grand picture palaces such as the Odeon in Kensington Church Street to the little cinemas of country towns, few of which now survive as cinemas, though many were converted into halls for playing bingo, a gambling game of eighteenth-century origin, which become extremely popular in the second half of the twentieth. Scores of theatres were going up too: the Saville Theatre in London, for example, in 1931; the huge New Theatre, now the Apollo, in Oxford in 1933. So were larger and larger shops. London's first Woolworth's was being built in Oxford Street in 1924, soon to be followed by numerous other stores of which D. H. Evans (1937) was a characteristic example.

To take shoppers and office workers home to their houses in the suburbs ever expanding around London – as they were round all other large towns – the lines of the underground railway were constantly being extended and new stations, such as those by Charles Holden on the Piccadilly Line to Hounslow, were being built in a style that evokes a vivid image of those days of the 1930s when Stuart Hibberd wore a dinner jacket to read the news at the recently built Broadcasting House, when George V's son, the future, unfortunate, King Edward VIII, could have been seen dancing with Mrs Dudley Ward at the Embassy Club, when Ivor Novello's *Glamorous Night* was delighting audiences at the Theatre Royal, Drury Lane, and there were long queues outside cinemas showing Shirley Temple in *Curly Top*.

To most of these pleasure-seekers of the 1930s the economic problems of the country seemed far away. Indeed, by the middle of the decade politicians were informing them, in the words of Neville Chamberlain, Baldwin's Chancellor of the Exchequer and soon to become Prime Minister, 'that we have recovered in this country 80 per cent of our prosperity'. The story of *Bleak House* was over, he announced, and the people could now sit down to enjoy the first chapter of *Great Expectations*.

Churchill in characteristic attire.

Soon afterwards the Italian Fascist dictator, Benito Mussolini, invaded Abyssinia and the German Chancellor, Adolf Hitler, reoccupied the Rhineland of which Germany had been deprived by the 1919 Treaty of Versailles, whose harsh terms had made a future European war almost inevitable. In 1938 German troops entered Austria; in 1939 they seized Czechoslovakia; then Hitler turned upon Poland; and Chamberlain, who had done all he could to avoid fighting by a policy of appeasement, was obliged to declare war on Germany, whose well-trained army crossed the Polish frontier on 1 September after Hitler had signed a non-aggression pact with Russia.

Children trying out their gas masks at the beginning of the Second World War.

Chamberlain was not the man to lead his country in such a crisis; and Churchill, his First Lord of the Admiralty, took over as Prime Minister, directed the fortunes of his country with erratic brilliance for five years, and at the general election of 1945 was heavily defeated at the polls by voters anxious that Britain should not return to the politics of the 1920s and 1930s when Churchill, as Home Secretary at the time of the General Strike, had misguidedly referred to the workers as 'the enemy'.

A 1940 poster praising the achievements of the Royal Air Force, in the words of Winston Churchill speaking in the House of Commons on 20 April 1940.

The leader of the Labour Party which now came to power – with an absolute majority in the House of Commons for the first time in its history – was Clement Atlee, a restrained, laconic man who might well have been mistaken for the manager of a small bank and whose great gifts were so well concealed by a veneer of imperturbable diffidence that Churchill is supposed, in a characteristic judgement not intended to be taken seriously, to have described him as 'a sheep in sheep's clothing'.

His government – in which the reassuringly bulky figure of Ernest Bevin was Foreign Secretary, the ascetic Sir Stafford Cripps President of the Board of Trade, and the fiery Welsh orator, Aneurin Bevan, Minister of Health – set about their task with invigorating energy, introducing a series of Bills in fulfilment of promises to nationalize essential industries and the means of supply, to lay the foundations of what became known as the Welfare State and to bring back some measure of prosperity to a country where rationing was as severe as it had been during the war. The government also began to restore the havoc caused by air raids which had damaged or destroyed no fewer than 3,500,000 houses in London alone as well as laid waste such national treasures as Coventry Cathedral, which was rebuilt to the designs of Sir Basil Spence.

By 1951, the centenary of the Great Exhibition and the year in which the Conservatives under Winston Churchill were returned to power, so much had been done that the government decided to hold a Festival Exhibition on derelict land on the south bank of the Thames in Lambeth 'to demonstrate to the World the recovery of the United Kingdom from the effects of War in the moral, cultural, spiritual and material fields'. The Press derided the pretension of this claim, but the Festival was visited by nearly ten million people; and the Royal Festival Hall – 'the first major public building in inner London designed in the contemporary style of architecture' – remains a fitting memorial to the enterprise. Subsequent public buildings on the South Bank, notably the Hayward Gallery and Denys Lasdun's National Theatre, have not been so well received.

For thirteen years after their re-election in 1951, the Conservatives were in power. They were years of growing prosperity; wages were far higher than they had been before the war though prices had risen very little; more and more people were buying cars and going on holidays. 'Let's be frank about it,' the Prime Minister declared in 1957, 'most of our people have never had it so good.' By the 1960s Britain was one of the world's leading industrial as well as nuclear powers.

... WE'VE GOT **HIM** !

Caricature of Harold Macmillan, Prime Minister in the late 1950s.

This world was now divided between a communist east and a capitalist west, with various uncommitted nations hovering uneasily between the two and an international body with headquarters at New York, the United Nations, endeavouring to settle the differences between them. When in 1950 the communist North Korea invaded the South, which was supported by the United States, sixteen members of the United Nations, including Britain, sent troops to defend the South and helped to bring the war to an inconclusive end. In 1956 another war was brought to an end when – under pressure from the United States – British troops were obliged to withdraw from Egypt where, in alliance with France and in collusion with Israel, they had landed in an effort to bring about the fall of the Egyptian President, Gamal Abdel Nasser, who had recently nationalized the Suez Canal.

The Suez adventure, which brought about the fall of Anthony Eden, Churchill's successor as leader of the Conservative Party, was an anachronistic display of imperialism. Churchill had declared in 1942 that he had 'not become the King's First Minister in order to preside over the liquidation of the British Empire.' Yet during the intervening years the Empire had dissolved all the same. India and Pakistan gained their independence in 1947, Burma in 1948; Newfoundland joined the Dominion of Canada in 1949; several former African colonies emerged into state-

Margaret Thatcher, Conservative Prime Minister from 1979 to 1990, won the 1983 election after victory in the Falklands War.

In 1981 the tensions of inner-city life were highlighted by riots in the Toxteth area of Liverpool.

hood. Soon few of Britain's old colonial possessions were left, and most of these were being claimed by other countries. Gibraltar, captured from them in 1704, was being claimed by the Spanish; Hong Kong, ceded by them in 1842, by the Chinese; the Falkland Islands, a crown colony since 1892, by the Argentinians whose army launched an attack upon them in 1982, an attack vigorously resisted by the Conservative Prime Minister, Margaret Thatcher, who – calling an election after the immensely expensive British victory – won another victory for the Conservatives, their most decisive for forty years.

Margaret Thatcher was the sixth Prime Minister the country had had since Eden had resigned in 1957 in favour of Harold Macmillan, an almost theatrically patrician figure who, like his successor, the kind, modest and old-fashioned Sir Alec Douglas-Home, seemed peculiarly out of place in a country becoming known for its 'permissive society'. The governments of none of Mrs Thatcher's predecessors, neither those of the Labour leaders, Harold Wilson and James Callaghan, nor that of the Conservative Edward Heath, had succeeded in finding a satisfactory answer to the economic and industrial problems of the country or to the celebrated complaint of the American Secretary of State, Dean Acheson, that Britain had lost an Empire but not yet found a new role. It was an observation voiced also by the French President, General de Gaulle, who believed that Britain was too closely involved with the United States to make a satisfactory member of the European Economic Community established by the Treaty of Rome in 1957. Twice de Gaulle vetoed Britain's application for membership of the Community which she had declined to join upon its foundation; and it was not until January 1973, during the premiership of that zealous advocate of European co-operation, Edward Heath, that she was admitted to membership at last. Yet the British people remain equivocal about the Community.

Mrs Thatcher, single-minded and didactic, unswerving in her belief in self-reliance and what has come to be known as privatization, was determined that Britain should lose as little as possible of her sovereignty, and that, to use her own words, she should 'recover her self-confidence and her self-respect'. Much was achieved under her leadership, which was brought to a sudden end by her own party in 1990. She was succeeded by the comparatively little-known John Major, who won an unexpected victory in the general election of April 1992. However, his administration was dogged by misfortunes and by increasingly bitter divisions in his own party over Europe, and in May 1997 a newly confident Labour Party, under the leadership of the youthful modernizer Tony Blair, was swept into power with a huge majority.

The European flag adopted by the European Community in 1986.

By the beginning of the 1980s the English were falling behind in the world race. In 1964 they had produced more per head of population than any of the countries in the European Community except West Germany. In 1977 they produced less than any other except Italy. Had it not been for the discovery of oil in the North Sea the economic decline would have been even sharper. While those in work continued to prosper, unemployment was high and there were social as well as economic problems that seemed intractable, problems posed by increasing pollution, by crime and violence, by unassimilated immigrant communities, racial and class prejudice and the decay of the inner cities, problems soon to be compounded by rising inflation. As always, much remains to be done by future governments, while Britain's role in Europe remains a question to be resolved.

It is fortunately not required of historians that they should be prophets, only that by explaining the past they may provide lessons for the future, since history takes its revenge upon those who ignore it. At least some knowledge of the outlines of England's history and achievements may lead us to hope that, for all the afflictions of modern society, the English are even now, as Milton suggested they were over 300 years ago, 'not beneath the reach of any point that human capacity can soar to'.

Anglesey

Liverpool

Beaumaris

Conway

Ellesmere Port

Chester

Caernarfon

Stoke-on-Trent

Longton

Llangollen

Harlech

Shrewsbury

Ironbridge

Ludlow

Worcester

Cardigan

Hereford

Brecon

Gloucester

Carmarthen

Pembroke

Chepstow

Berkeley

Swansea

Caerphilly

Cardiff

Bristol

Bath

Bradford-on-Avon

Steeple Ashton

Wells

Glastonbury

Barnstaple

Huish Episcopi

Taunton

Cadbury Castle

Yeovil

Exeter

Dorchester

Maiden Castle

Tintagel

Launceston

Wadebridge

Plymouth

Truro

Penzance

0   30 miles

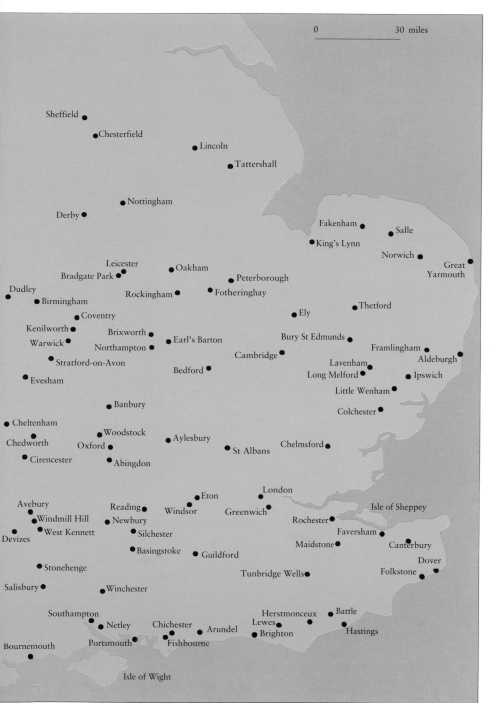

0   30 miles

Sheffield

Chesterfield

Lincoln

Tattershall

Nottingham

Derby

Fakenham

Salle

King's Lynn

Norwich

Great Yarmouth

Leicester

Oakham

Peterborough

Bradgate Park

Dudley

Rockingham

Fotheringhay

Birmingham

Ely

Thetford

Coventry

Kenilworth

Brixworth

Bury St Edmunds

Warwick

Northampton

Earl's Barton

Framlingham

Aldeburgh

Stratford-on-Avon

Cambridge

Lavenham

Bedford

Long Melford

Ipswich

Evesham

Little Wenham

Banbury

Colchester

Cheltenham

Woodstock

Aylesbury

Chelmsford

Chedworth

Oxford

St Albans

Cirencester

Abingdon

London

Eton

Avebury

Reading

Windsor

Greenwich

Isle of Sheppey

Windmill Hill

Newbury

Rochester

Devizes

West Kennett

Silchester

Faversham

Canterbury

Basingstoke

Guildford

Maidstone

Dover

Stonehenge

Tunbridge Wells

Folkstone

Salisbury

Winchester

Southampton

Herstmonceux

Battle

Netley

Chichester

Lewes

Arundel

Hastings

Bournemouth

Portsmouth

Fishbourne

Brighton

Isle of Wight

Berwick-upon-Tweed ●

0 _____ 30 miles

Lindisfarne (Holy Island)

Bamburgh ●

Alnwick ●

Hadrian's Wall

Newcastle upon Tyne ●

●Carlisle

Durham ●

Darlington ●

Whitby ●

Grasmere ●

Richmond ●

●Kendal

Rievaulx ●

Jervaulx ●

Scarborough ●

Ripon ●

Fountains ●

Harrogate ●

York ●

Blackpool ●

Bradford ●

Leeds
(Kirkstall Abbey)

Beverley ●

Kingston upon Hull ●

●Preston

Wakefield ●

Blackstone Edge ●

Grimsby ●

Manchester ●

Doncaster ●

Liverpool ●

Sheffield ●

●Chesterfield

●Chester

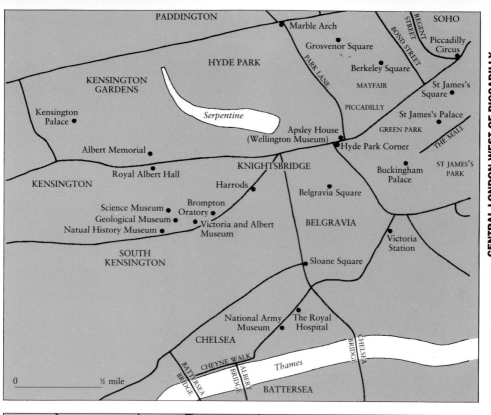

CENTRAL LONDON WEST OF PICCADILLY

CENTRAL LONDON EAST OF PICCADILLY

Marston Moor 2 July 1644

Preston 17-19 Aug 1648

Adwalton Moor
2 June-13 July 1643

Winceby Sept-8 Dec 1643

Chester

Nantwich 29 Jan 1644

Newark

Shrewsbury

Leicester

Naseby 11 May-14 June 1644

Warwick

Worcester 3 Sept-15 Oct 1651

Hereford

Copredy Bridge 23 May-29 June 1644

Edgehill
12-23 Oct 1642

Banbury

Chalgrove Field 18 June 1643

Roundway Down
13 July 1643

Oxford

Brentford and Turnham Green
24 Oct 1642-Jan 1643

Bristol

Newbury 20 Sept 1643
and 17-27 Oct 1644

Maidstone
1 June 1648

Lansdown
3-24 July 1643

Cheriton 29 March 1644

Langport 16 June-10 July 1643

Stratton 16 May 1643

Exeter

Lostwithiel 10 Aug-5 Sept 1644

0 _____ 50 miles

● Cathedral

△ Country House

Seaton Delaval △

● Carlisle

Durham ●

△ Rydal Mount
Brantwood

Ripon ● Castle Howard △

Allerton Park △

● York

△ Burton Agnes

Harewood House △

● Liverpool

△ Chatsworth

Chester ● Hardwick Hall △ Lincoln
Little Moreton Hall △ Southwell ●

Wollaton Hall △

Holkham Hall
Sandringham ● △

Shugborough △ Harlaxton △
Manor Houghton Hall ●

Blickling Hall

Lichfield ● Burghley House △ Peterborough ●

Norwich ●

Hagley Hall △

Coventry ● Ely ●

Charlecote Park △

Worcester ● Holdenby △

Hereford ● △ Woburn Abbey

St David's ● Sezincote △ Sulgrave Manor △

Gloucester ● Blenheim Palace △
● Oxford ● St Albans

Kelmscott △ Hughenden △ Claremont △

Lacock Abbey △ London ●

Bristol ● Bath ● △ Littlecote Rochester ●

Wells ● Longleat △ Guildford ● Canterbury ●

Stourhead △ Salisbury Winchester
Montacute △ Wilton ● △ Mottisfont Abbey

Chichester ● Brighton
Pavilion △
Petworth
△

Exeter ● Osborne House

Truro ●

0 ———————— 50 miles

Anglo-Saxon Kings

Up to c.800 the most important kings only are listed; from the reign of Egbert onwards a succession emerges of kings who are effectively rulers of the whole of England

Aelle, King of Sussex (? late 5th century)
Ceawlin, King of Wessex (560-91/2)
Aethelbert, King of Kent (560-616)
Redwald, King of East Anglia (?-616/27)
Edwin, King of Northumbria (616-33)
Oswald, King of Northumbria (634-42)
Oswy, King of Northumbria (642-70)
Egfrith, King of Northumbria (667-85)
Pendu, King of Mercia (? 632-55)
Wulfhere, King of Mercia (658-674)
Aethelred, King of Mercia (674-704)
Caedwalla, King of Wessex (685-8)
Ine, King of Wessex (688-726)
Wihtred, King of Kent (692-725)
Cenred, King of Mercia (704-9)
Ceolred, King of Mercia (709-16)
Aethelbald, King of Mercia (716-57)
Ceolwulf, King of Northumbria (729-37)
Offa, King of Mercia (757-96)
Aethlred, King of Northumbria (774-9, 790-6)
Beohtric, King of Wessex (786-802)
Conwulf, King of Mercia (796-821)

Egbert (802-39), King of the West Saxons
Ethelwulf (839-55), son of Egbert, King of the West Saxons and Kentishmen
Ethelbald (855-60), son of Ethelwulf, King of the West Saxons
Ethelbert (860-6), son of Ethelwulf, King of the West Saxons and Kentishmen
Ethelred I (866-71), son of Ethelwulf, King of the West Saxons and Kentishmen
Alfred the Great (871-99), son of Ethelwulf, King of the West Saxons
Edward the Elder (899-924), son of Alfred, King of the Angles and Saxons
Athelstan (924-40), son of Edward, King of the West Saxons and Mercians
Edmund (940-6), son of Edward, King of the English
Edred (946-55), Son of Edward, King of the English
Edwy (955-9), son of Edmund, King of the English
Edgar (959-75), son of Edmund, King of the English
Edward the Martyr (975-8), son of Edgar, King of the English
Ethelred II, the Unready (979-1016), son of Edgar, King of England
Edmund Ironside (1016), son of Ethelred, King of England

House of the Skjöldings, or of Denmark

Canute (1016-35), King of the English, Danes and Norwegians
Harthacanute and Harold I, Harefoot (1035), sons of Canute,
Kings of Denmark and England
Harold I, Harefoot alone (1035-40)
Harthacanute again (1040-2)
Edward the Confessor (1042-66), son of Ethelred, King of England
Harold II Godwinson (1066), King of England

Normans and Plantagenets 1066 - 1485

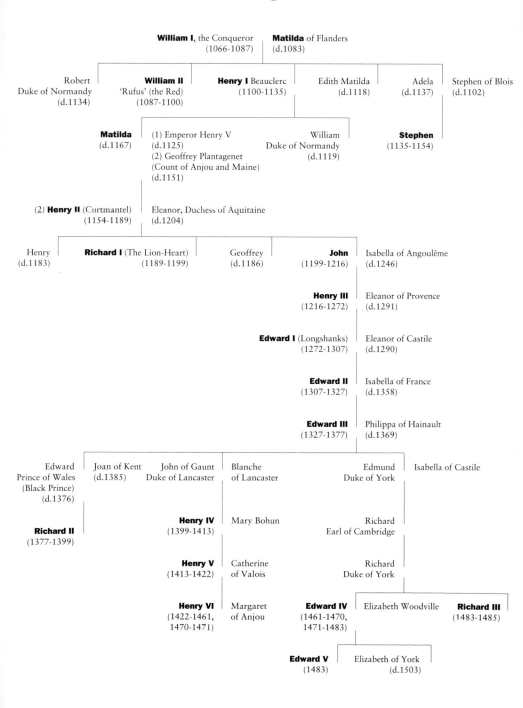

William I, the Conqueror (1066-1087) — **Matilda** of Flanders (d.1083)

Robert, Duke of Normandy (d.1134)

William II 'Rufus' (the Red) (1087-1100)

Henry I Beauclerc (1100-1135)

Edith Matilda (d.1118)

Adela (d.1137) — Stephen of Blois (d.1102)

Matilda (d.1167) — (1) Emperor Henry V (d.1125) (2) Geoffrey Plantagenet (Count of Anjou and Maine) (d.1151)

William, Duke of Normandy (d.1119)

Stephen (1135-1154)

(2) **Henry II** (Curtmantel) (1154-1189) — Eleanor, Duchess of Aquitaine (d.1204)

Henry (d.1183)

Richard I (The Lion-Heart) (1189-1199)

Geoffrey (d.1186)

John (1199-1216) — Isabella of Angoulême (d.1246)

Henry III (1216-1272) — Eleanor of Provence (d.1291)

Edward I (Longshanks) (1272-1307) — Eleanor of Castile (d.1290)

Edward II (1307-1327) — Isabella of France (d.1358)

Edward III (1327-1377) — Philippa of Hainault (d.1369)

Edward Prince of Wales (Black Prince) (d.1376)

Joan of Kent (d.1385)

John of Gaunt, Duke of Lancaster — Blanche of Lancaster

Edmund, Duke of York — Isabella of Castile

Richard II (1377-1399)

Henry IV (1399-1413) — Mary Bohun

Richard, Earl of Cambridge

Henry V (1413-1422) — Catherine of Valois

Richard, Duke of York

Henry VI (1422-1461, 1470-1471) — Margaret of Anjou

Edward IV (1461-1470, 1471-1483) — Elizabeth Woodville

Richard III (1483-1485)

Edward V (1483) — Elizabeth of York (d.1503)

The House of Tudor

John of Gaunt
Duke of Lancaster
(d.1399)

(3) Katherine Swynford
(d.1403)

John Beaufort
Earl of Somerset
(d.1410)

Margaret Holland

John
Duke of Somerset
(d.1444)

Margaret of Bletso

(1) **Henry V**
(1413-1422)
(2) Owen Tudor
(d. 1461)

Katherine of Valois
(d.1437)

Margaret Beaufort
(d.1509)

(2) Edmund Tudor
Earl of Richmond
(d.1456)

Edward IV
(1461-1470,
1471-1483)

Elizabeth Woodville

Henry VII
(1485-1509)

Elizabeth of York
(d.1503)

Henry VIII
(1509-1547)

(1) Catherine of Aragon
(m.1509 - div.1533 - d.1536)
(2) Anne Boleyn
(m.1533 - ex.1536)
(3) Jane Seymour
(m.1536 - d.1537)

Margaret Tudor
(1489-1541)

James IV of Scotland
(d.1513)

(1) **Mary I**
(1553-1558)

Philip II
of Spain
(d.1598)

(2) **Elizabeth I**
(1558-1603)

(3) **Edward VI**
(1547-1553)

James V of Scotland
(d.1542)

Mary
Queen of Scots
(1542 - ex.1587)

(1) Francis II of France
(d.1560)
(2) Henry, Lord Darnley
(1545-1567)

(2) **James I**
(James VI of Scotland)
(1603-1625)

Stuarts and Hanoverians 1603-1837

James I
(James VI of Scotland) (1603-1625)   Anne of Denmark (d.1619)

Henry
Prince of Wales
(d.1612)

Elizabeth
(d.1662)

Frederick V
Elector Palatine
of the Rhine
(d.1632)

Charles I
(1625-1649)

Henrietta Maria
dr of Henry IV of France
(d.1669)

Charles II
(1660-1685)

Katherine
of Braganza
(d.1705)

James II
(1685-1688)
(d.1701)

(1) Anne Hyde
(d.1671)
(2) Mary of Modena
(d.1718)

Mary
(d.1660)

William
of Orange

(1) **Mary II**
(1689-1694)

William III
(Son of Mary and
William of Orange)
(1680-1702)
(r. alone from 1694)

(1) **Anne**
(1702-1714)

George of Denmark
(d.1708)

Sophia
(d.1714)

Ernest Augustus
Elector of Hanover
(d.1698)

(2) James Francis
Edward Stuart
(Old Pretender)
(d.1766)

George I
(1714-1727)

Sophia Dorothea of Celle
(d.1726)

Charles Edward
(Young Pretender)
(d.1788)

George II
(1727-1760)

Caroline of Brandenburg-Anspach
(d.1737)

Frederick
Prince of Wales
(d.1751)

Augusta of Saxe-Gotha-Altenburg
(d.1772)

George III
(1760-1820)

Sophia Charlotte
of Mecklenburg-Strelitz
(d.1818)

George IV
Regent from
1811
King from
1820-1830

Caroline
of Brunswick-
Wolfenbüttel
(d.1821)

Frederick
Duke of York
(d.1827)

William IV
Duke of Clarence
(1830-1837)

Adelaide
of Saxe-Meiningen
(d.1849)

Edward
Duke of Kent
(d.1820)

Victoria
of Saxe-Coburg
(d.1861)

Charlotte
(d.1817)

Victoria
(1837-1901)

Descendants of Queen Victoria

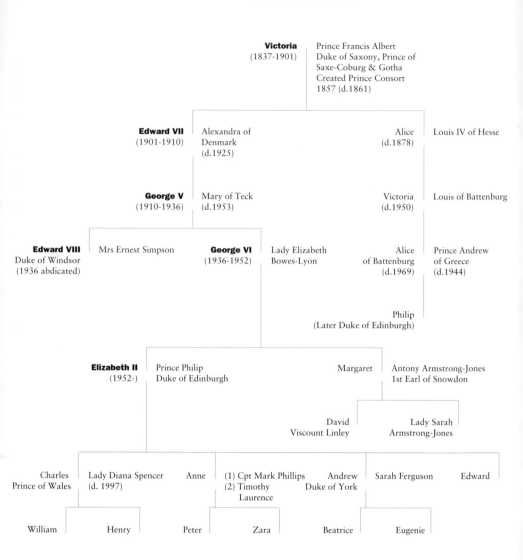

Victoria
(1837-1901)

Prince Francis Albert
Duke of Saxony, Prince of
Saxe-Coburg & Gotha
Created Prince Consort
1857 (d.1861)

Edward VII
(1901-1910)

Alexandra of
Denmark
(d.1925)

Alice
(d.1878)

Louis IV of Hesse

George V
(1910-1936)

Mary of Teck
(d.1953)

Victoria
(d.1950)

Louis of Battenburg

Edward VIII
Duke of Windsor
(1936 abdicated)

Mrs Ernest Simpson

George VI
(1936-1952)

Lady Elizabeth
Bowes-Lyon

Alice
of Battenburg
(d.1969)

Prince Andrew
of Greece
(d.1944)

Philip
(Later Duke of Edinburgh)

Elizabeth II
(1952-)

Prince Philip
Duke of Edinburgh

Margaret

Antony Armstrong-Jones
1st Earl of Snowdon

David
Viscount Linley

Lady Sarah
Armstrong-Jones

Charles
Prince of Wales

Lady Diana Spencer
(d. 1997)

Anne

(1) Cpt Mark Phillips
(2) Timothy
Laurence

Andrew
Duke of York

Sarah Ferguson

Edward

William

Henry

Peter

Zara

Beatrice

Eugenie

WORLD CHRONOLOGY

- 2660 BC First pyramid built
- c2500 BC Menhir statues of Sardinia and Southern France
- 2330-2180 BC 6th Egyptian dynasty
- 1972 BC Jubilee shrine at Karnak
- 1972 BC Hammurabi accedes to the throne in Babylon
- c1750 BC Hammurabi's 'Eye for an Eye' law code
- c1595 BC Hittites take Babylon
- c1400 BC Destruction of Knossos
- c1290 BC The Temple of Abu Simbel begun
- c1250 BC Agamemnon, King of Mycenae, leads Greeks against Troy
- c970 BC Death of Solomon, King of Israel
- 776 BC First Olympic Games
- 753 BC Traditional date of founding of Rome by Romulus and Remus
- 594 BC Solon Archon at
- 558-529 BC Cyrus the ruler of the Persian Em

- 490 BC Greeks at Mar
- c479 BC Dea
- 458 BC Aes
- 430-404 BC
- c429 BC S
- 411 BC Ar
- c405 BC F
- 399 BC T
- 347 B
- 323
- 322
- 2

BRITISH CHRONOLOGY

- c5000 BC-2500 BC Neolithic Britain
- c3250 BC West Kennet Long Barrow built
- c2500 BC-1600 BC Early and Middle Bronze Ages
- c2200 BC -1300 BC Stonehenge built
- 2000 BC-1600 BC Avebury Stones erected
- c2000 BC Immigration of Beaker Folk
- c1600 BC-AD 43 Iron Age
- c1000 BC First hill forts built
- c800 BC Immigration of Celts

BC 0 AD · · · · · · 200 · · · ·

lefeat Persians   • 27 BC-AD 14 Octavian (Augustus) first Roman Emperor

hon   •AD 30 Jesus of Nazareth condemned to death

of Confucius   • 64 Rome burned in time of Nero and Christians persecuted

ylus' *Oresteia*   • 70 Destruction of the Temple in Jerusalem

Peloponnesian War between   • 79 Destruction of Pompeii and Herculaneum by eruption of Vesuvius

Athens and Sparta   • 80 Colosseum dedicated

hocles' *Oedipus Rex*   • 98 Tacitus' *Life of Agricola*

tophanes' *Lysistrata*   • 105 Chinese invent paper

ripides' *Bacchae*   • 110-11 Juvenal's satires

ial of Socrates   • 111-14 Trajan's Forum built

Death of Plato   • 116 Trajan conquers Assyria and Mesopotamia

C Death of Alexander the Great   • 117-38 Reign of Hadrian

C Death of Aristotle   • 124 Pantheon built at Rome

4 BC Beginning of Punic Wars between   • 135 Capture of Jerusalem

Rome and Carthage   • 161-80 Reign of Marcus Aurelius

218 BC Hannibal crosses the Alps   • 216 Baths of Caracalla built in Rome

c214 BC Great Wall of China finished   • 267 Athens sacked by Germ

206 BC-AD 220 Han dynasty in China   • 284-305 Reign of Diocl

• 179 BC Basilica Aemilia built in Rome   • 306-37 Reign of

Athens   • 59 BC Julius Caesar appointed Consul   • 330 Cor

reat   • 53 BC Vercingetorix leads revolt against Romans in Gaul

ire   • 44 BC Caesar assassinated

• c143 Antonine Wall in Scotland begun

• 185 Antonine Wall abandoned

• 195-7 Usurper emperor Albinus in Britain

• 197 Barbarians overrun Hadrian's Wall

• c208 Hadrian's Wall rebuilt by Septimius Severu

• 287-296 Carausius and A

• 306 Constantine th

• 100 BC Immigration of Belgae

• 55 BC Julius Caesar's first expedition to Britain

• 50 BC Cassivellaunus, British chieftain

• AD 43 Roman invasion

• 49 Foundation of Colchester

• c50 Foundation of London

• 51 King Caractacus defeated

• 61 Rebellion of Iceni under Boudicca

• 70-84 Conquest of Wales and north

• c75 Fishbourne Palace built

• 78-c85 Agricola Governor of Britain

• 122 Hadrian's Wall begun

• c140 Theatre built at Verulamium (St Albans)

400 · · · · **600** · · · ·

- 410 Visigoths sack Rome
  - 450 Metal stirrup in use in Asian steppes
  - 453 Death of Attila the Hun
  - 455 Vandals sack Rome
    - 469 Visigoths begin conquest of Spain
      - 511 Death of Clovis, King of the Franks
        - 523 Boethius' *Consolation of Philosophy*
        - 529 Benedictine Order founded
          - 537 Haghia Sophia finished in Constantinople
            - 619-906 Tang Dynasty in China
              - 625 Mohammed begins dictating Koran
                - 652 Pagoda of the Great White Goose,
                  - 674 Arabs attack Constantinople
                    - 711 Arabs land in Spain
                      - 751 Earlie

Heruls
an
onstantine
antine founds new city of Constantinople
- 376 Visigoths cross Danube
  - c397 Saint Augustine's *Confessions*

- 735 Death of Bede
  - 757 Offa

ectus usurper emperors in Britain
Great proclaimed Emperor at York
- 407 Constantine the Third proclaimed Emperor in Britain
- 409 Last Roman legions leave
  - c446 Romano-British make last appeal for help from the Emperor Valentinian
  - c450 Contact between Rome and Britain severed
  - c450 Hengist and Horsa settle in Kent
    - c455 Hengist rebels against Vortigern
      - c470 Saxons settle in Sussex
        - c495 Saxons settle in Wessex
          - c510 Battle of Mount Badon
            - 597 Arrival of St Augustine
              - 664 Synod of Whitby
                - 668 Arrival of Archbishop Theodore
                  - 672 Synod of Hertford
                  - c672 Rise of Mercia
                    - c698 Lindisfarne Gospels

- 910 Foundation of Benedictine Abby at Cluny
- 911 Rollo the Viking becomes first Duke of Normandy
- 933 Foundation of Delhi
- 962 Otto I crowned Holy Roman Emperor
- 987 Accession of Hugh Capet in France
- 992 Langeais Castle built in the Loire valley, France
- 992 First commercial treaty between Venice and Byzantium
- 997-1004 Building of St Martin at Tours
- 1035 William the Bastard becomes Duke of Normandy

sian
- 1055 Seljuk Turks at Baghdad

t printed book, Buddhist *Diamond Sutra*
- 788 Great Mosque at Cordoba begun
- 800 Charlemagne crowned Emperor of West
- 860 Russians besiege Constantinople
- c870 Invention of gunpowder in China
- 880 Foundation of Kiev
- 885 Normans besiege Paris
- 889 Angkor founded

becomes King of Mercia
- c793 First Viking raids on Britain
- c800 *Beowulf*, Old English epic poem
- 829 Northumbrians submit to Egbert, King of West Saxons
- 867 Northumbria falls to Danes
- 870 St Edmund murdered
- 871 Accession of King Alfred
- 878 Alfred defeats Danes
- 886 Danelaw established in Northern England
- c891 Anglo-Saxon Chronicle begun
- 960 St Dunstan becomes Archbishop of Canterbury
- 973 Edgar acknowledged as their overlord by British princes
- 991 Danegeld first levied
- 1016 Cnut chosen as King
- 1042 Edward the Confessor becomes King
- 1065 Westminster Abbey consecrated
- 1066 Battle of Hastings

WORLD CHRONOLOGY

- 1661 Louis XIV absolute ruler of France
- 1664 Ottoman Turks occupy Hungary
- 1669 Crete ceded by Venice to Ottomans
- 1670 Molière's *Bourgeois Gentilhomme*
- 1670 Hudson's Bay Company founded
- 1674 Jan Sobiewski elected King of Poland
- 1677 Racine's *Phèdre*
- 1683 Turks besiege Vienna
- 1685 Revocation of Edict of Nantes
- 1703 Peter the Great founds St Petersburg
- 1715 Death of Louis XIV; ac
- 173.

BRITISH CHRONOLOGY

- 1660 Restoration of the Monarchy: Accession of Charles II
- 1664-5 Great Plague
- 1666 Great Fire
- 1667 The Dutch in the Medway
- 1674 End of War against Dutch
- 1685 Accession of James II
- 1688 Glorious Revolution
- 1689 Accession of William III and Mary II
- 1701 War of Spanish Succession begins
- 1702 Accession of Anne
- 1704 Battle of Blenheim
- 1707 Union of England and Scotland
- 1714 Accession of George I
- 1715 Jacobite rebellion
- 1720 South Sea Bubbl
- 1727 Accessio

ART, ARCHITECTURE AND LITERATURE IN ENGLAND

- 1660 Royal Society constituted
- 1667 Milton's *Paradise Lost*
- 1675 Wycherley's *Country Wife*
- 1678 Bunyan's *Pilgrim's Progress*
- 1681-2 Dryden's *Absalom and Achitophel*
- 1687 Newton's *Principia Mathematica*
- 1694 Bank of England established
- 1700 Congreve's *The Way of the World*
- 1705 Blenheim Palace begun
- 1710 St Paul's Cathedral complete
- 1710 Defoe's *Robinson Crusoe*
- 1726 Swift's G
- 1729 Pope
- 173

1750   1800

• 1786 Mozart's *Marriage of Figaro*   • 1836 Bat
   • 1789 French Revolution
     • 1795 Mungo Park explores Niger
     • 1796 Bonaparte's Italian Campaign
      • 1798 Haydn's *Creation*
      • 1804 Beethoven's *Eroica Symphony*
        • 1808 Goethe's *Faust*
        • 1808-14 Peninsular War
          • 1812 Napoleon's retreat from Moscow
          • 1813 Napoleon defeated at Leipzig

ession of Louis XV to French throne   • 1817 Venezuela independent un
Ch'ien-lung becomes Chinese Emperor   • 1827 Battle of Nava
• 1741 Frederick the Great defeats Austrians   • 1828 Death of Sch
   • 1755 Lisbon earthquake   • 1830 Revolutior
     • 1770 Cook sights Australia   • 1832 Greek

of George II   • 1805 Battle of Trafalgar   • 1838 /
• 1742 Fall of Robert Walpole   • 1811 Luddite disturbances   • 1838-
   • 1745 Jacobite rebellion   • 1815 Battle of Waterloo   • 184
     • 1756 Seven Years' War begins   • 1819 Peterloo massacre
     • 1757 Battle of Plassey   • 1820 Accession of George IV
      • 1759 Quebec captured   • 1820 Cato Street conspiracy
      • 1760 Accession of George III   • 1825 Trade unions lega
       • 1763 Peace of Paris   • 1829 Catholic En
         • 1773 Boston Tea Party   • 1832 Great Re
         • 1776 American Declaration of Independence   • 1833 Factory
          • 1780 Gordon Riots   • 1833 Beginni
          • 1781 Surrender at Yorktown   • 1833 Slavery
           • 1783 Americans win independence   • 1834 Trans
           • 1784 Wesley founds Methodist Church   • 1836 Cha
            • 1803 War with France   • 1837 Ac

• 1742 Handel's *Messiah*   • 1821 Constable's *Hay Wair*
   • 1749 Fielding's *Tom Jones*   • 1824 National Gallery
     • 1753 British Museum founded   • 1829 Stephenson
      • 1761 Sterne's *Tristam Shandy*   • 1831 Faraday
       • 1767-74 Bath, Royal Crescent built   • 1832 Tennyso
       • 1768 Royal Academy founded with   • 1837 Fir
         Sir Joshua Reynolds as its first President   • 1839
       • 1769 Watt's steam engine
         • 1776 Gibbon's *Decline and Fall of the Roman Empire*
         • 1776 Smith's *Wealth of Nations*
           • 1796 Vaccination against smallpox
liver's Travels   • 1798 Malthus's *Essay on Population*
Dunciad   • 1805 Wordsworth's *Prelude*
5 Hogarth's *Rake's Progress*   • 1813 Austen's *Pride and Prejudice*
• 1741 Richardson's *Pamela*   • 1819-24 Byron's *Don Juan*

• f the Alamo | • 1861-5 American Civil War • 1879 Edison's electric light | • 1917 USA enters W
44 French war in | • 1862 Turgenev's *Fathers and Sons* • 1882 Daimler's petrol engine | • 1917 Russian Rev
Morocco | • 1864 Pasteur invents pasteurization • 1888 Van Gogh's *Sunflowers* | • 1922 Muss
1847 Liberia becomes | • 1865 Lincoln assassinated | • 1894 Dreyfus Case | • 1924 De
independent | • 1867 Typewriter invented | • 1895 Marconi's wireless | ass
1848 Communist Manifesto | • 1867 Marx's *Das Kapital* | • 1896 Chekhov's *The Seagull* | • 192
• 1850 Taiping rebellion | • 1869 Suez Canal opened | • 1898 Curies discover radium | •
• 1851 Verdi's *Rigoletto* | • 1870 Franco-Prussian War | • 1900 Boxer Rebellion
• 1851 Melville's *Moby Dick* | • 1873 Tolstoy's *Anna Karenina* | • 1904 Freud's *Psychopathology* | •
• 1852 Napoleon III | • 1874 First Impressionist Exhibition | *of Everyday Life*
Bolivar proclaimed Emperor | • 1876 Bell's telephone | • 1905 Russian-Japanese War
• 1856 Flaubert's *Madame* | • 1876 Wagner's *Ring* cycle performed | • 1905 Einstein's theory of relativity
rt *Bovary* | • 1876 Degas's *Dancing Class* | • 1905 Cézanne's *Les Grandes Baigner*
Paris • 1860 Garibaldi proclaims | • 1879 Dostoyevsky's *The Brothers* | • 1907 Picasso's *Les Demoiselles d'*
ependence Victor Emmanuel King of Italy | *Karamazov* | • 1915 D.W. Griffith's *Birth of*

Corn Law League | • 1885 Gordon killed at Khartoum | • 1
irst Afghan War | • 1893 Irish Home Rule Bill rejected by Lords | •
nny Post | • 1896 Sudan conquered
846 Repeal of Corn Laws | • 1899 Second Boer War
• 1848 Chartist movement collapses | • 1901 Accession of Edward VII
• 1851 Great Exhibition | • 1904 Anglo-French entente
d • 1854 Crimean War | • 1909 Employment Exchanges i
ipation • 1857 Opium War | • 1911 First National Health
n Bill • 1857 Indian Mutiny | Insurance Bill
• 1868 Disraeli becomes Prime Minister | • 1914-18 First World W
f Oxford Movement • 1868 Gladstone's first Liberal government | • 1916 Battles of Som
lished in British Empire • 1876 Queen Victoria becomes Empress of India | • 1917 Battle of Pass
ation of 'Tolpuddle Martyrs' • 1879 Zulu War | • 1919 Treaty of
movement launched • 1880 First Boer War | • 1924 Fir
ion of Queen Victoria • 1882 Occupation of Egypt | • 1926

• 1855 Trollope's *The Warden* | • 1913 Lawrence's *Sons an*
ided • 1859 Darwin's *Origin of Species* | • 1919 Shaw's *He*
ocket • 1860 Barry's Houses of Parliament completed | • 1921 Ruther
overs electrical induction • 1868-9 Browning's *The Ring and the Book* | • 1922 Eliot's
Lady of Shalott • 1871 Royal Albert Hall | • 1922 Joyce
lliam Museum built • 1872 George Eliot's *Middlemarch* | • 1926
ner's *Fighting Temeraire* • 1878 Morris's *The Decorative Arts*
44 Disraeli's *Coningsby* | • 1892 Wilde's *Lady Windermere's Fan*
1847 Charlotte Brontë's *Jane Eyre* | • 1894 Shaw's *Arms and the Man*
1847 Emily Brontë's *Wuthering Heights* | • 1895 Henry Wood starts Promenade Concerts
1847 Thackeray's *Vanity Fair* | • 1896 Hardy's *Jude the Obscure*
• 1848 Macaulay's *History of England* | • 1899 Elgar's *Enigma Variations*
• 1848 Mill's *Principles of Political Economy* | • 1901 Kipling's *Kim*
• 1849 Dickens's *David Copperfield* | • 1903 Liverpool Cathedral begun
• 1851 Ruskin's *Stones of Venice* | • 1904 Conrad's *Nostromo*

ar
ution
ini's March on Rome
th of Lenin: Stalin
mes power in Soviet Union
-9 Le Corbusier's Villa Savoie
29 Hemingway's *A Farewell*
    to Arms
29 Wall Street Crash

- 1945 Yalta Conference
- 1945 Atomic bomb
- 1947 Independence for India, Pakistan, Burma
- 1949 People's Republic of China proclaimed
- 1949 NATO founded
- 1950 Outbreak of Korean War
- 1952 Beckett's *En attendant Godot*
- 1953 Death of Stalin
- 1957 Treaty of Rome

- 1933 Hitler becomes Chancellor
- 1937 Picasso's *Guernica*
- 1939 Franco captures Madrid

es
- 1941 Welles's *Citizen Kane*
vignon
- 1941 Pearl Harbor
Nation
- 1944 Liberation of Paris

- 1958 De Gaulle President of France
- 1962 Cuban Missile Crisis
- 1963 Kennedy assassinated
- 1963 Vietnam War begins
- 1966 Chinese Cultural Revolution begins
- 1967 Six-Day War

- 1968 Russian invasion of Czechoslovakia
- 1969 First man on Moon
- 1979 Afghanistan war begins
- 1980 Iran – Iraq war begins
- 1985 Gorbachev assumes power in USSR
- 1986 US bombs Libya
- 1989 Tiananmen Square massacre
- 1989 Berlin Wall pulled down
- 1990 Iraq invades Kuwait
- 1991 Gulf War

---

29 Vote for women over 21
929 Second Labour government
1931 National government led by Ramsay Macdonald
1931 Gold standard abandoned
- 1938 Chamberlain and Hitler at Munich
- 1939-45 Second World War
troduced
- 1940 Battle of Britain
- 1940 Churchill becomes Prime Minister
- 1940 Withdrawal from Dunkirk
r
- 1942 Battle of El Alamein
e and Jutland
- 1944 D-Day invasion of France
hendaele
- 1945 Labour government under Attlee
ersailles
- 1951 Festival of Britain
Labour government
- 1956 Invasion of Suez
General Strike
- 1959 First motorway

- 1969 North Sea oil discovered
- 1973 Joined European Common Market
- 1974 Miners' strike
- 1980 Self-sufficiency in North Sea oil
- 1981 Social Democratic Party founded
- 1982 Falklands War
- 1983 Conservatives re-elected under Mrs Thatcher
- 1987 Mrs Thatcher wins third term of office
- 1990 Mrs Thatcher resigns; John Major becomes Prime Minister

---

Lovers
rtbreak House
rd and Chadwick split the atom
The Wasteland
Ulysses
aird invents television
1930 Waugh's *Vile Bodies*
- 1932 Broadcasting House built
- 1935 Watson-Watt devises radar
- 1935 Epstein's *Ecce Homo*
- 1937 Whittle invents jet engine
- 1940 Greene's *Power and The Glory*
- 1945 Moore's *Family Group*
- 1949 Orwell's *1984*
- 1951 Martin's Royal Festival Hall

- 1953 Bacon's *Study after Velázquez's Portrait of Pope Innocent X*
- 1954 Amis's *Lucky Jim*
- 1956 Osborne's *Look Back in Anger*
- 1962 Coventry Cathedral consecrated
- 1976 Lasdun's National Theatre
- 1983 Burrell Collection Museum, Glasgow opened
- 1983 William Golding wins Nobel Prize for Literature
- 1986 Richard Rogers's Lloyds of London

Prime Ministers

Reign of King George II (1727-1760)

Robert Walpole	1727
Earl of Wilmington	1741
Henry Pelham	1743
Duke of Newcastle	1754
Duke of Devonshire	1756
Duke of Newcastle	1757

Reign of King George III (1760-1820)

Duke of Newcastle	1760
Earl of Bute	1762
George Grenville	1763
Marquess of Rockingham	1765
Earl of Chatham	1766
Duke of Grafton	1768
Lord North	1770
Marquess of Rockingham	1782
	(27 March)
Earl of Shelburne	1782
	(4 July)
Duke of Portland	1783
	(2 April)
William Pitt (the Younger)	1783
	(19 December)
Henry Addington	1801
William Pitt	1804
William Wyndham Grenville	1806
Duke of Portland	1807
Spencer Perceval	1809
Earl of Liverpool	1812

Reign of King George IV (1820-1830)

Earl of Liverpool	1820
(Tory)	
George Canning	1827
(Tory coalition)	(10 April)
Viscount Goderich	1827
(Tory)	(31 August)
Duke of Wellington	1828
(Tory)	

Reign of King William IV (1830-1837)

Duke of Wellington	1830
(Tory)	
Earl Grey	1830
(Whig)	(22 November)
Viscount Melbourne	1834
(Whig)	(16 July)
Duke of Wellington	1834
(Tory)	(17 November)
Robert Peel	1834
(Tory)	(10 December)
Viscount Melbourne (Whig)	1835

Reign of Queen Victoria (1837-1901)

Viscount Melbourne (Whig)	1837
Robert Peel (Tory)	1841
Lord John Russell	1846
(Whig)	

Earl of Derby	1852
(Tory)	(23 February)
Earl of Aberdeen	1852
(Tory Coalition)	(19 December)
Viscount Palmerston	1855
(Liberal)	
Earl of Derby	1858
(Conservative)	
Viscount Palmerston	1859
(Liberal)	
Earl Russell	1865
(Liberal)	
Earl of Derby	1866
(Conservative)	
Benjamin Disraeli	1868
(Conservative)	(27 February)
William Ewart Gladstone	1868
(Liberal)	(3 December)
Benjamin Disraeli	1874
(Conservative)	
William Ewart Gladstone	1880
(Liberal)	
Marquess of Salisbury	1885
(Conservative)	
William Ewart Gladstone	1886
(Liberal)	(1 February)
Marquess of Salisbury	1886
(Conservative)	(25 July)
William Ewart Gladstone	1892
(Liberal)	
Earl of Rosebery	1894
(Liberal)	
Marquess of Salisbury	1895

Reign of Edward VII (1901-1910)

Marquess of Salisbury	1901
(Conservative)	
Arthur James Balfour	1902
(Conservative)	
Henry Campbell-Bannerman	1905
(Liberal)	
Herbert Henry Asquith	1908
(Liberal)	

Reign of King George V (1910-1936)

Herbert Henry Asquith	1910
(Liberal coalition from May 1915)	
David Lloyd George	1916
(Liberal coalition)	
Andrew Bonar Law	1922
(Conservative)	
Stanley Baldwin	1923
(Conservative)	
James Ramsay MacDonald	1924
(Labour)	(27 January)
Stanley Baldwin	1924
(Conservative)	(4 November)
James Ramsay MacDonald	1929
(Labour coalition from 1931)	

Stanley Baldwin	1935
(Conservative)	

Reign of King Edward VIII (1936)

Stanley Baldwin	1936
(Conservative)	

Reign of King George VI (1936-1952)

Stanley Baldwin	1936
(Conservative)	
Neville Chamberlain	1937
(Conservative)	
Winston Churchill	1940
(Coalition)	
Clement Attlee	1945
(Labour)	
Winston Churchill	1951
(Conservative)	

Reign of Elizabeth II (1952-)

Winston Churchill	1952
(Conservative)	
Anthony Eden	1955
(Conservative)	
Harold Macmillan	1957
(Conservative)	
Alec Douglas Hone	1963
(Conservative)	
Harold Wilson	1964
(Labour)	
Edward Heath	1970
(Conservative)	
Harold Wison	1974
(Labour)	
James Callaghan	1976
(Labour)	
Margaret Thatcher	1979
(Conservative)	
John Major	1990
(Conservative)	
Tony Blair	1997
(Labour)	

Leaders of the Opposition since the Ministers of the Crown Act 1937

Clement Attlee	(1937-45)
Winston Churchill	(1945-51)
Clement Attlee	(1951-55)
Hugh Gaitskell	(1955-63)
Harold Wilson	(1963-64)
Edward Heath	(1965-70)
Harold Wilson	(1970-74)
Edward Heath	(1974-75)
Margaret Thatcher	(1975-79)
Michael Foot	(1980-83)
Neil Kinnock	(1983-92)
John Smith	(1992-94)
Tony Blair	(1994-97)
William Hague	(1997-)

BIBLIOGRAPHICAL NOTE

Perhaps the best of the one-volume histories of England which cover the ground more fully than this book has room to do is *The Oxford Illustrated History of Britain* (ed. Kenneth O. Morgan, 1984). Others that can be recommended are R. J. White's *A Short History of England* (revised edition, 1962), Paul Johnson's *A History of the English People* (revised edition, 1985), Jasper Ridley's *A History of England* (1981), Keith Feiling's *A History of England* (1950), E. L. Woodward's *A History of England* (third edition, 1965) and Hugh Kearney's *The British Isles : A History of Four Nations* (1989). Classic older works are Lord Macaulay's *History of England* (paperback edition, 1986) and G.M. Trevelyan's *A Shortened History of England* (paperback edition, 1987).

Three good generously illustrated books are F. E. Halliday's *A Concise History of England* (revised edition, 1980), John Burke's *An Illustrated History of England* (new edition, 1985), and David McDowell's *An Illustrated History of Britain* (1989).

Three recent social histories are Maurice Ashley's *The People of England* (1982), Asa Briggs's *A Social History of England* (1983) and my own *The English: A Social History, 1066-1945* (1987). Christopher Taylor has revised W. G. Hoskins's *The Making of the English Landscape* (1988).

For more detailed treatment, there is the splendid fifteen-volume *Oxford History of England* which is now being superseded by the *New Oxford History of England* of which the first volume, *A Polite and Commercial People: England 1727-1783*, appeared in 1989.

INDEX